After

Birth

Unconventional Writings

from the Mommylands

By Jenny Fiore

Published and distributed by
Possibilities Publishing
PO Box 10671
Burke, VA 22009
www.possibilitiespublishingcompany.com

Dedicated to Betty Vaughan,
the funniest writer you never knew

Contents

Uncut

Our boy is uncut. He still has his foreskin. Blam! People told us his penis would look weird if we didn't cut it. Fine, I'll admit it sort of looks like a solitary okra. But I wouldn't call it weird, considering that cut penises look like Prince Valiant. Go ahead. Check yours. Check your husband's. I'm right.

Like most parents, my husband and I started researching our son's penile options well before delivery day. We didn't do the quick-and-easy research that ends with *Gross, that's gonna get cheese!* Nor, unlike many folks, did we stop at *Check it out! Babies have magic penises that don't feel pain!* We just kept an open mind with a skeptic's edge.

There was certainly hygiene to consider, and on that point, pictures and anecdotes that erased Ricotta from my diet. There was susceptibility to diseases, particularly if our son were to ever one day pay for sex—not a thought we cared to entertain. The whole topic of pain was big (not just his physical pain, but my emotional pain). Diatribes about locker-room politics were bountiful. Not to be overlooked was the matter of son's penis matching daddy's—or not. Apparently this is really important. Which is weird, because I would never wish for my daughter to be my vagina clone.

My husband was working as a physician assistant in urology at the time. He'd seen a few penises. From his exam-room experiences, we talked about the cut-to-uncut ratios; the numbers were barely disparate. We talked about complications with both options: intractable foreskins and botched circumcisions, for example. Apparently you can totally reconstruct a movie star's face, but the head of a wiener is really hard to fashion. Even the lead urologist, when asked his professional opinion, proved to be ambivalent.

The cut and uncut seemed to be in a dead heat. So, we turned to the crystal ball, trying to gauge what the future held for penises (other than higher salaries). We read up on statistics and trends across the nation, finding circumcision of newborns to be in the minority and on the decline on the coasts. The Midwest, where we live, was holding firm ground with truckfuls of foreskins in the circumcision camp. If we circumcised our son, would life be easier for him in the Midwest? And if so, would it be unethical for us to hack his peter beret to ensure he always stayed close to us? (Did I say that last part out loud?)

I didn't really go so far as to imagine how his foreskin would one day affect his job mobility, but I did go so far as to imagine how it would one day affect his sex life. Rumor has it that penises aren't just locker room decorations anymore but are actually used in poking things for pleasure. Oddly enough, I found very little discussion about this topic as I scoured the Internet and canvassed fellow parents. Apparently, nobody wants to acknowledge that their kids are one day going to have sex.

What I did next was one of the most selfless things I have ever done as a parent—because it was for the benefit of my child's future sex life, and therefore I can never tell him I did it. Who on earth wants to hear that his mom Googled "uncut + fellatio" on his behalf? Also, a preponderance of evidence from other more seasoned mothers tells me there's a very, very strong likelihood I won't *want* him to enjoy sex with the person he chooses to have it with. And yes, I meant to say *person* instead of *people*. That's how mommy wants it to be, selfless mommy Googling "circumcised + penis + smell + sex."

I'm not a dirty birdy. I promise. I'm actually a big non-fan of sexual explicitness. *Keep it in your bedroom* is my motto (except in my own bedroom, where it's *keep it in your pants*). So, Googling things like "orgasms + circumcision" isn't exactly my idea of a fun Saturday night. Yet I did.

Performing my informal research, I lurked in chat rooms where people discussed openly their preferences about penises. I checked out what gay men had to say and what straight women had to say. Did they have a preference in the bedroom? What was it and why? Did partners shy away from oral sex with uncut men? Did they prefer it? I asked heaps of questions, getting interesting information about the sexual pleasure partners derived from uncut penises—as well as the pleasure they witnessed uncut men experiencing. And, yes, though it wasn't monumental, there certainly seemed to be a difference.

Armed with all the information we could gather, we finally made our decision. The scale wasn't tipped completely to one side, but for us, like our son's future penis, it *was* tipped. Sure, one friend told me right off the bat that my son's uncut penis looked weird. (So does her kid's face, but you don't hear me talking about it.) Sure, I marveled at the thing myself. Yes, I've had people gawk a little during diaper changes. But I'm in the Midwest, remember, and my son is now solidly, anatomically designed for the coasts—like George Clooney.

So, in a nutsack—I mean nutshell, I went to the heart of the matter. The penis *is* a sex organ. Not being Jewish or otherwise formally bound to circumcision, I felt that researching the whole sex aspect was a no-brainer. No man wants his parents deciding how sensitive his penis is going to be during sex, or figuring his odds for receiving a blow job from a nice Jewish girl. Yet every man was once a boy, and every boy's parents must make those decisions. I'll never get to tell my son about the horrible pop-ups, graphic discussions, and humiliating pictures I waded through to ensure his future sexual pleasure, but in a way I wish he could know. Because if that isn't selfless parenting? If that ain't love? I don't know what is.

Dance Review: Mom as Critic

This week, I review *What the What?*—the latest installment in the Random Acts mini-ballet series being performed in the Unfinished Basement Theater. Intrigued by the string of invitations I received from the prima ballerina over the course of an hour yesterday afternoon, the show seemed worth a look. She insisted it was the company's best production yet, not to be missed. The admission fee of a meager $2.00 at the door seemed reasonable, and her assurances had left me hopeful that good dance theater doesn't have to be costly.

I was wrong.

Initially the female principal dancer lingered gloriously, effortlessly responsive to the hard, high notes of a sonata apparently playing in her head. She darted around and across the stage with high-speed, high-definition clarity. But to call the performance wholly engrossing would be a grave exaggeration: She seemed, at times, indecisive and lacking control of her appendages. It was unclear whether her gelatinous execution of pirouettes was intentional.

Were her Parkinsonian movements merely a product of the all-too-predictable unpredictability of improvisational dance? Methinks no. The cataclysmic execution of her movements by mid-production was curiously painful to watch, much like the live birth of a horse.

The female lead did have an arresting gift for altering speed, regardless of the lack of musical accompaniment. In that regard, she took real risks. She certainly didn't dance small. Yet, for all the physical space she filled, her performance never felt expansive. It didn't light up the heights and depths of the theater.

The costumes, on the other hand, rendered me hugely entertained. A portion of the program was performed with the male lead in the nude, and this reviewer certainly had never before seen how the male appendage responds to the centrifugal force of a pirouette, however small the appendage and however poorly executed that pirouette might be. Unfortunately, the gratuitous nudity of the male lead eclipsed the few, hopeful sequences in which the female lead stretched up in yearning arabesques, only to fall away in epileptic movements that were surely meant to communicate something profound. In the second act, the costumery was incongruous: the female lead majestically dressed in Christmas finery (over pants) and the male lead wearing a cheap wig and a long-sleeved ringer tee with a basketball patch. It was unclear why.

As for the lead male role, it was not danced with especial distinction; and crucial aspects of style required for improvisational dance were rendered poorly. The dancer appeared confused, if happily so, and it was unclear whether he had even received formal training or the benefit of rehearsal before the show went live. Nonetheless, I couldn't look away. I was captivated by the bright chaos of his movement even as his failed attempt at accompanying the performance with a plastic saxophone solo was, quite simply, sad.

Finally, the setting—a concrete-slab room—presumably chosen for its minimalist appeal, was merely depressing, even prison-like. Visions of Abu Ghraib came to mind. It smelled of cat litter, an olfactory twist that I can't say worked in the way I assume the stage designers planned.

It's unfortunate to say that apoplectic choreography, imprecise execution, and perplexingly random pageantry are not infrequent with this particular dance company.

One-half star.

Worship

She sits in the row in front of me, because *he's* there. The boy is blonde with blue eyes, and that's all that matters to a six-year-old brunette with hazels. She doesn't see the cowlicks, doesn't want to run her fingers against her tongue and press the rogue hairs down the way I do. He's on his knees but not praying with the rest of us. He's using the pew as a desk, coloring on the back of the church bulletin. Blue, green, red, and yellow colored pencils are piled like pick-up sticks on the floor around him, amounting to her favorite thing, a rainbow.

The gentleman preacher is teaching about the Lord's Prayer, parsing the phrases into small bits in scholarly fashion. And because the one-room Sunday school isn't open today, she's getting the etymology lesson right along with me. I mean she *would* be getting it, if not for the blue eyes and cowlicks and rainbow of pencils. But who am I kidding? Even without him, she'd be dying of boredom— dying a slow, demonstrative, hunchbacked death of sighs.

The little boy's dad rips out a sheet of drawing paper and passes it down the row to her. She looks back at me for approval, which I give without so much as a word or movement. It's something she seeks and finds in my eyes. On the paper, she draws a picture of a mouth with square teeth in a row, like Chiclets, and circles the front two. "My Loose Toth Poster," she chicken-scratches across the top. Then she slides the paper around on the chair like a dropped handkerchief, hoping the boy will see it. She knocks at her barely loose front tooth—her first ever— with her fingernails and the pencils. She holds the paper up close to her face and then throws her head back and shuts her eyes deliciously. *Oh, God, it's the ecstasy of St. Teresa!* The boy doesn't even notice. He's a *boy*.

As the church fills with the music of a piano, she unearths an empty purple balloon that was spirited into her pocket before we left the house. It's meant to hold water, so it's the size and shape of a tiny guppy. I make a certain dark and disapproving thing happen with my eyes, and I see disappointment flash in her own. *A balloon was the very thing the boy would have liked.* My wrinkled old finger reaches over her shoulder and turns to the correct page in the hymnal. "It goes first line, first line, first line," I whisper. "Then second line, second line, second line. Then third line, third line, third line."

She nods, partly to avoid trouble, partly to let the boy know she really knows how to read all those lines, even the words like *vesture* and *descendeth*. He doesn't care. He's a *boy*.

"Are there any prayer requests?" the preacher asks. She shoots me an uncertain look, a question of whether her head must bow. I wink at her, and she purses her lips and nods in gratitude. *Thank you, Mom, for giving me this hair-fine thread of permission to be human and move freely about the cabin.*

"Nanny!" she whisper-yells at me over her shoulder. She wants to request a prayer for her great-grandmother. I tell her to go ahead, but it's like giving her permission to drive the car; she doesn't know how. I ask her what she wants, and she whispers through her cupped hand, "Pray for Nan, because she's old and in the hospital and dying."

Nan is 94 but in a nursing home, not a hospital, and I stop short of telling her we're *all* dying. Not just because I have a heart but also because she is picking her nose. In front of the blue-eyed boy, she has zoned out with her pointer trying to swirl and hook a booger, and I feel sorry for her.

I raise my hand and say, "My daughter wants to put in a request for her great-grandmother, who is in a nursing home and sometimes gets lonely."

Put in a request? I think. *Like I'm putting in an order for fries?* I'm embarrassed and my hands start to shake as I smooth out the bulletin on my lap. Public speaking gives me the sweats. My daughter is smiling proudly at the boy. He didn't hear her thoughtful prayer request. He's a *boy.*

When the golden offering plates are passed, she couldn't be more thrilled. "Mom!" she whisper-yells. "Can I put the money in the plate?"

I don't have a dime, not even a pen to fill out a check. *Jesus Christ, kid, shhhhhhhaaaad up.* I can't give her a dark look, because people are watching now. So, I lie. I lie in the House of the Lord and tell her that we write a *check* for our offering and only *one a month.* I don't have time to explain that we make offerings only when mommy has spare cash on her. No time to explain why mommy treats the church like a hobo. Besides, she only wanted the boy to see her do it. Like a boy would actually care.

As the last hymn rises up, the woman next to me rattles

18

everyone's bones with her Beverly Sills booming soprano finale. My daughter looks back at me again, this time to see if it could be me who's making that impressive sound. She points a hopeful finger to ask, and I do that thing with my eyes again but also throw in a little thing with my jaw, and she stops cold. She knows it means *turn around*. If only it had been me that sang like a bird, maybe the boy would have noticed.

She sits down and clicks her fingernail against the loose tooth again, harder and harder and harder. She spins the drawing around under her finger. She flips through the pages of the hymnal. Nothing is working. Finally she pulls the balloon from her pocket again, starts to look back at me, but realizes my eyes are going to do that thing again. So, she stops her eyes from meeting mine and instead settles them on the boy, putting the balloon between her loose teeth. Surer than salvation, he drops everything.

He sat next to a girl at church, and he didn't listen to his dad's whispered warnings. *Sit down. Pay attention. We're almost done.* How could he? She was a brunette with hazel eyes and held an empty purple water balloon in her teeth.

Not That Mom

"Who wants Pizza Pockets!?"

Into the kitchen a mob of sweaty teenagers comes, one with a basketball under his tanned arm. He kisses the pretty lady on the cheek as she pulls off her plaid oven mitts. "Thanks, Mom!" he says as he and his sweaty friends grunt toward the baked dough pockets, stuffing them into their cheeks like coked-up hamsters.

The pretty lady looks at the camera and gives a knowing smile, a really big one but with no teeth showing. Nothing makes her happier than being the cool mom with fresh-baked snacks that can lure the whole gang over to her place, all of them wishing she were *their* mom.

I am not that mom.

Into my front door a mob of ratty-haired kindergartners comes, and I'm tired of their needs before they even shut the door behind themselves. (Not really. They never shut the door behind themselves!) From the time the first

Jibbitz-packed Croc comes off the first little foot, I begin to dispense rules to my daughter: "Only in the basement or your room, and clean up your mess when you're done." I also tell her, "Don't you dare ask me to feed this impoverished nation of midgets you've brought to my house." I don't say that part with my mouth, but I say it with my *eyes*.

Then it starts, the endless stream of requests made without question marks or manners:

"Mrs. F, I'm *hungry.*"

"Libby's Mom, I'm *thirsty.*"

"Hey, we can't move this play kitchen outside through the rain and into the fort by *ourselves.*"

These are not my children. I will ignore their passive-aggressive pleas. I really will. Because that play kitchen is made of untreated wood that will rot in a week outside. And have you seen my grocery bill lately, my darling sponges? You want a snack at my house, you damn well better ask for one directly—with a smile—and a *please*. Because I am not UNICEF, kiddos, and you are not from a war-torn country with a food shortage. I don't say this stuff with my mouth. I say it with the hairs on my neck, how they stand up, crest-like. I'm a very subtle Dilophosaurus.

But the TV commercials keep telling me I should try to make my kids' friends fall in love with me, and I should do so by reheating frozen foods from cardboard containers and bobbing my hair. They tell me I should do this while wearing a V-neck and khakis instead of a worn-out tee and a broom skirt with Taco Bell beans on it. They tell me that these things will lead my spawn to be the sort that *still* kisses me on the cheek, unprompted, when 17 years old. They don't say it with their mouths. But still.

And it's tempting. I admit it's tempting. I'd love to do my daughter proud, be the Girl Scout troop leader, the one with the apples already cut before the school bell rings, laid out in a ring like I'm expecting a kinder-cocktail party. It might be nice to be *that mom*, so I admit I fantasize sometimes—when I'm not in front of a mirror bearing witness to the dog pile that's my coif—that maybe I could pull it off. Just a little extra effort, right?

Yes. Even though the kids are barking orders like Fidel

Castro and ringing a goddamn cowbell in the living room—not my daughter's bedroom and not the basement, like I asked—I suppose I should get them those Hot Pockets and Kool-Aid now. And I really will, just as soon as I finish hoisting this play kitchen onto my back and hauling ass into the rain.

Dear Husband

I give up.

If you want me, take me as I am...

...in my over-lined fat-smothering bathing suit at 6:30 p.m., with black beans smeared down the bosom, and my hair pulled back in a chlorinated ponytail that, thankfully, was at least "washed" a little in the hot tub. Finally.

...with mascara smeared under my eyes even though I haven't cried OR showered OR applied makeup within the last 24 hours. How does that happen? I know it's there and makes me look vaguely like Amy Winehouse; I just don't have any place glamorous to go with a baby and a 5-year-old, and why not do my part in helping some other slightly less disheveled mom feel superior for a spell?

...with a pubic hair or two growing midway between my groin and knee. I don't know what the hell they're doing there either, but my choices today were to either shave them or wash a load of whites so you'd have some clean undershirts. Verdict? Nobody will get a glimpse of *your* hairy nipples tomorrow at work, thank you very much.

…with breath that smells vaguely like the cat litter. Which is to say that I both need to brush my teeth AND clean the cat litter. I *know.*

…with nothing particularly riveting to say. You're not exactly Oliver Sacks or David Sedaris all the time either, you know. Well, actually, I know you know. I'll settle for silently looking at the stars together if you will. And I know you will. Thank you.

…with a million neuroses, from having to check Craigslist for rectangular white-wood dinettes 27x per day to having to point out every time you have a booger anywhere in my line of vision, even if it's microscopic. What can I say? I'm reliable.

…with a chunk of cantaloupe/cheese/applesauce stuck in my hair. The baby threw it there while I was cleaning the floor under his high chair *again,* and removing it *again* would have involved work *again* as well as the ability to fantasize that I was going to see anybody but the kids and you today. Sorry, but I chose to write about it rather than attend to it. What's new?

…with Internet OCD. No, I suppose it's *not* really wise for me to take my turn in Facebook Scrabble or to look up *verticillium fungicides for ash trees* at 10:59 p.m., just as my eyes were getting heavy in bed, but I can't get on the computer during the day for more than 60-second bursts without the baby going berserker trying to pry the shift bar loose. And if I hadn't made my desperate little digital foray into the World Outside at that time, I would have been up doing it around 2 a.m. instead. We both know that.

…with too many crow's feet now to cover up with line-filler. They're mostly from you anyway, from being so thoroughly entertained and made to laugh so much since I met you. Even when I stink. Even when I'm sad. Even when I'm annoying the holy hell out of you. Would I sound like Glenn Close in *Fatal Attraction* if I said that we're meant to be? You know we are.

Just so you know, I'm not really giving up on myself, dear. I'm just really ready for school to start. T minus five days and counting. Then I'm getting a little bit of me back, and so will you. I promise.

But I'm still not giving up the ponytail.

Kind of a Big Deal

My child is more special than everyone else's children.

Five years ago, I gave birth to a beautiful, brilliant, and most likely Messianic creature that looked, well, a little better than the other babies in the nursery ward. The nurses were professional about it, but I could tell whenever they brought the baby to me for feedings that they were exercising more care than usual. Obvious to me, from the way they sort of lingered before completely releasing her into my cradled arms, the nurses knew this was *one of the special ones.*

My sweet darling had a little trouble nursing at first, but

thank goodness I was able to convey to the hospital staff the *urgency* and *seriousness* of our need to meet with the lactation consultant. Though she had to be pulled from another patient's room, I knew that once she saw my child, she would understand why I could not be persuaded to wait.

My daughter breezed—no, absolutely *stormed* – through her milestones. In those early years, nary an hour passed without discussion about it. I would be talking to people in checkout lines or at the bank, and of course, the topic would always somehow turn to my extraordinarily interesting child. They might offer up this or that tedious anecdote about their own children, now adults or teenagers or middle-schoolers, but amazingly, my experiences with my daughter were always more interesting, more profound, and more prominent in these discussions. No doubt these people had heard plenty of stories about when little So-and-So first walked, funny things little So-and-So said, issues with So-and-So's adenoids, but I'm certain these stories paled against my own. Beautiful, intuitive, possibly a savant or one of those "indigo children," my daughter was just someone that warranted a lot of excitement.

When it came time for preschool registration, we were horrified to learn that our child did not receive a priority placement and was instead put on a waiting list! Clearly certain factors needed to be brought to light, for example our financial pliability and willingness to serve on the advisory board as well as volunteer as dishwashers and snack-preparers—essentially whatever was necessary. Thank God we gained access through a friend of a friend to the preschool director. And thank God we were able to slip ahead of that poor *autistic* child that had previously topped the waiting list. Of course, we assume in light of his—well, in light of him—that he could afford to wait a year or semester. We hate to say it, but it was far more critical that our child's special talents be brought to fruition as quickly as possible. So, the front of the line for us it was!

Now that my daughter's in kindergarten, I'm discouraged by the lack of personalized attention she receives. We recently had a parent/teacher conference, to which we brought a small notebook of questions (e.g., when can we have her tested by the gifted and talented program director?), constructive criticism (e.g., wouldn't sliced fresh strawberries be a more appropriate morning snack than

Goldfish crackers?), diagrams (e.g., a brilliant re-order of the current classroom seating arrangement, to relocate our daughter away from the less savvy non-readers), and photographs (just because we knew the teacher would not believe all the cute things our child does at home!). Well, I'll be darned if the teacher didn't keep us to some horrible, standardized boilerplate for conferences—a mere 20 minutes. For God's sake! As if those parents in the hallways couldn't be asked to wait a little longer for their turn!

Recently we began receiving notes from the teacher about our daughter's "behavioral issues." As if our child can be expected to wait in a line when she's not at the front of it! Doesn't this so-called blue-ribbon teacher realize our daughter is the shortest student and can't tolerate having her line of vision obstructed? That's what the private-practice occupational therapist we hired said, at least. Apparently, it's a spatial thing. I've heard it's an early marker for leadership skills, as well. And really? Our wonderfully independent child has to wait for permission after she asks to get a drink? She has to sit down when told? She can't physically act out her frustration whenever someone else is Student of the Week? What is this? Communism?!

This morning on our way to school, I had to slip our minivan around the car in front of us at the four-way stop in order to shave 30 seconds off our travel time and avoid the inconvenience of waiting for others. Passing on the right in a school zone may not be legal, but an exception should be made for those of us who are, well, *a priority*. Of course, once we got to the campus, I then had to again slip my minivan around to the front of the line in the roundabout because, well, leaders don't wait! I lingered maybe a little longer than usual, but this was to make sure my daughter's fresh strawberries were secured in her BPA-free snack kit.

I don't really care if it bothered those rule-followers behind me, with their ordinary children and their ordinary lives. What was that front space for, if not for people with higher priorities and more special children than the others?

I have learned that rules are made to be broken in the name of special, special people—like us. Everyone seems to be forgetting we're kind of a big deal.

Deus ex Machina

I kneel at the altar of the Internet. I do this, quite literally, dozens of times a day. My legs folded under the rest of my body, my arms reaching out in front of me like a Muslim readying to touch my forehead to the holy mat that is my keyboard, I open myself to answers and messages. When I need to know the weekend weather, when I need to find a movie time, when my daughter wants to know *the name of that scary dinosaur* in an old audiobook we heard called *Little Blue*, I can always find the answer on the Internet. Aside from the universe itself and mankind's existential and spiritual questions about it, I know of no other thing so vast as the worldwide web.

Before the Internet, the closest thing I had to it was a set of encyclopedias my parents kept on a bookshelf in my childhood living room. Though it housed the complete clearinghouse of world facts available to the modern family at the time, there was nothing particularly God-like about it. The shelf *was* a somewhat glorified hub for our home, much like the computer work area to the 21st century family. It fit into a corner of the living room and was our largest piece of furniture. I can vividly remember minute details about it, like the bumpy parts where the sanding was shoddy. It held some of my geologist dad's favorite finds on it—pyrite, turquoise, a cracked-open geode. It also held my parents' snazzy stereo and LPs, including Stevie Wonder's *Songs in the Key of Life,* my mom's double-LP Jane Fonda Workout, and a Chuck Mangione specimen with close-ups of Chuck's jeans as he jumped on a trampoline. But the lowest of the three shelves was the reason the shelf was built in the first place, for our encyclopedias.

Our encyclopedias were green leather with gold lettering on their spines. They took up one-and-a-half walls, just like the shelf designed to hold them. As I do now with the Internet, I satisfied boredom now and again with the encyclopedias, opening them up randomly to read about whatever happened to be there. I read about diseases and foreign countries and names of chicken breeds and types of wood-boring beetles. It was like hitting Wikipedia's "Random article" link, except the random knowledge I'd accumulate was a little more alphabetical in nature. I'd learn gobs about stuff that started with the letters *Ab-* for a while. By the next month, I'd be keen on trivia starting with *Br-*.

Yet I never worshipped at the altar of the Britannicas. Back then it was okay, and commonplace, to settle for *not* being able to find an answer on demand. From anyone at all, a shrug was a perfectly acceptable answer to trivial questions. We didn't run to the encyclopedias to *know* everything.

Now, in the age of search engines, I can't seem to settle for a shrug. Most of us can't. Which might sound like progress, but do I really need to confirm for myself in the middle of lunch with my four-year-old that the Native American actor in *Dances with Wolves* shares a name with the famous Brit who wrote the *Third Man*? And why?

A dozen or more times a day, my daughter sees me going to the computer for answers. When she asks whether she needs mittens for school, I go to the weather sites. When she wants to know what the new president looks like again, I do a Google image search. We've even spent time in front of the screen with her spouting off random requests for visuals:

"Monkey with a camel!"

"Rainbow over a unicorn!"

"Bunnies in a nest!"

"Dog using a toilet!"

It never disappoints. Never. Explaining the life cycle of butterflies was easier with the computer than with the actual larvae that lived in a netted cube in her room. We've checked out potential houses together online. I've shown her the kindergarten she'll be attending. Pictures of my hometown? No problem in cyberspace. Everything, every answer, every triviality and incarnation of any and everything seems to be held in the computer. *Deus ex machina*. God from the machine.

What is this doing to my young child? To all the kids? Do they know, at age three, age four, age five, that life's answers aren't given to us by some God-like thing *within* the computer? Do they realize God isn't quite literally *in* that machine?

This oddly disturbing thought first struck me years ago

when my husband was deployed to Kuwait. I was showing my daughter, then two years old, the location of Kuwait relative to our Wisconsin home, using Google Earth.

"This is a picture of the world from far, far away," I said. "This is where we live, and over heeeeeeere is where Daddy is."

She leaned toward the computer, put her mouth within earshot of Kuwait and somewhat hollered, "Hi, Daddy!"

"Oh, no, honey," I explained. "He's not *in* there. This is just a picture." She looked at me with something like distrust. I'd just said, 'This is where Daddy is." Now I was saying he wasn't there. More important, before that moment, a simple Internet search had never let us down. It was Mommy's Great and Powerful. So, why the heck wasn't Daddy in there?

Because of what I'd done, and still do, my daughter could imagine the computer capable of housing a whole, missing man. She must imagine it houses so much more. On the bookshelf in my childhood living room, I saw the finite nature of man's accumulated knowledge. It started with an A and ended with a Z. How will our young kids gather the same about our computers?

My Pets

I love my kids. I love them just as much as childless people love their pets. They *are* my pets. I know that folks who've gone through the blood, sweat, and tears of owning actual pets get irritated when I say this, but it's true. My children mean as much to me as any dog or cat means to its parent. We are bonded in the very same way.

Most pet-owners would lay down their lives for their feathered and furry babies. Call me crazy, but I'd do the same for my children. I honestly understand what it feels like. It's an almost primal feeling, like the one that forms in the Humane Society adoption center when you're pretty sure you're going to adopt that wiener dog. When a person walks out those doors with the signed papers, she knows in her bones she'd both live for and die for what's tugging at that leash, so I can't help but draw comparisons. I don't know how else to explain what I felt when I left the hospital with the six-pound creature that came out of my vagina and couldn't even hold its—I mean *her*—cute little head up.

I have not been out on a single New Year's Eve since my first baby was born. How is that not like owning a cat? Nights like that one, babysitters are almost as hard to come by as pet-sitters. But like a cat-owner, I just tell myself *it's not all about me*. I turn in early and lay awake waiting for the sounds of fireworks and gunshots at midnight. Because I know my kids are going to wake and freak just like dogs do. See? I get it. Maybe I don't know what it's like to have to give them a Xanax in those moments and massage the pill down their throats, but I'd sure like to try.

I know many people who bottle-fed their puppies or kittens, night after sleepless night, but I'd have done the same for my babies if I could have. Just because they drank hundreds of gallons of milk and a full bra-cup size from my breasts, that doesn't mean I don't care about them just as much as if I'd wrestled for their nourishment with one of those infuriating string closures on the top of a pet food bag. All I have to show for it is saggy tribal boobs, which I know does not compare to can-opener-elbow, but still. And what of the fact that I used to pump milk from my body every couple of hours if I was going to be away from them for any length of time? That is just about as close as you can get to coming home between quitting time and bar time to feed a dog.

You know how lots of people get unsightly stretch marks and extra fat from having dogs? I swear to God, I have the same thing from having kids. Just as those pet-owners would happily gain another depressing 30 pounds and lose more elasticity in their skin to have those dogs again, I think I can say I'd probably do it all over again for my kids, too. Probably.

I estimate I've changed only thousands of diapers filled with a cornucopia of colors, odors, textures, and various corn kernels over the past seven years, which when you think about it, isn't that much easier than cleaning out the litter box once every day for years on end. Once I pet-sat for a goldfish, and trust me, I know how dirty a goldfish aquarium can get. I've picked up my fair share of dog poop with plastic bags, too. All of which is to say that I don't make these comparisons lightly. No, I know in my bones the love that survives explosive diarrhea. Just one more reason I consider my kids my pets.

Every time a war starts, every time there's threat of catastrophe, the common sentiment everywhere is this:

"How am I going to explain this to my dog?" With kids, your thoughts can fly to that hard place, too. As a pet-owner, you may say, "I don't know if I should even bring another cat into this world." But then something beautiful happens, like your four-legged blessing from God teaches you a little something about the meaning of life, and then it breaks your heart in a sort of wonderful way. Sometimes my kids do that to me. They're really just pets masquerading in skin.

You know what else? I sort of feel like I'm responsible for keeping my kids warm and safe and happy, for making sure they feel worthy of love, respect, and friendship, for keeping them out of jail and off drugs, for teaching them about compassion and sexual responsibility, and for helping them face frightening things like death, leaving home, and news stories about serial rapists. It's not quite as big a responsibility as teaching a dog not to eat its own feces or jam its nose into strangers' crotches, but it's similar.

After my babies grew inside my body, the product of a love shared between my husband and me, and after I pushed them out in painful, glorious labor, you know what I thought? I thought, "Holy crap. I feel like I just adopted a dog."

I don't care what people say. I really do love my kids just as though they were my pets.

Boys Will Be Boys

The fireman opens the door and hoists him into the truck. He tethers the small body into the seat, the shoulder strap going across my son's fragile neck. My son looks up at him with furrowed brow, as if to say, "I can strap my own goddamn seatbelt." Which he can. My son looks across to where I am sitting. Were he not two years old and small as a Cocker Spaniel, our knees would be nearly kissing. Instead, his small feet just reach the edge of the seat, and they make a lower-case V in their little hiking boots. They're the only clean thing about him.

We go around the block, and my daughter is giddy as she's asked to make the sirens go off by pushing down on something black on the floor. The back of his seat to hers, my son gazes out the window with something like seriousness. *This is men's business,* his face says. *I have places to go.* Large, yellow combines in the soy and corn fields around our neighborhood are laying bare the land. I wonder if the farmers are tired of hearing the sirens as the day's demonstration continues. My son isn't looking at the fields; he's surveying them. While sitting in a fire truck. He's studying combines ripping parched crops from their rows. His meaty hands look swollen as they press down on the seat. *Places to go.*

Afterward, we go into the fire station and sit amid crowds of people eating cheap hot dogs that look like the fat fingers of dying men. My son rips his hot dog out of the bun and throws the foil aside. He tears at the meat with his teeth and washes it down with water stolen from my daughter's cup. Then he gets on the ground and pulls at an old piece of vinyl, his face reddening and shaking with exertion. *Leave this to me,* his expression says.

There is an old couple sitting across from us. I'm pretty sure they're farmers, because they look like farmers. The man has an overbite of yellow teeth. His skin is parched, and his CAT ball cap is sitting high on his head, like someone set it there without him knowing. He's laughing at my boy. It's a hearty laugh, a Skoal laugh, the laugh of a man who has just shot a big buck or watched his boy clean a fish for the first time. He walks away and comes back with a pile of napkins. He plops them in front of my son and says, "How 'bout some napkins, feller?"

My son picks up a paper cup to wash more meat down his gullet, and finding the cup empty, throws it across the table. It hits the man's wife in the face, and as I'm apologizing and pulling my son's hands down to his lap, the old man laughs a proud laugh and says, "Boys will be boys." He couldn't be more delighted.

My son is two, but already I see him being welcomed into the boys' club. Whenever he destroys something or calls out to a dump truck or steps on a bug or turns away disinterestedly from a flower someone has shown him, faces light up. Men cross their arms and smile knowingly. When he falls, the sympathy is smaller. When he throws or jumps, the expectations are higher. He pees on things and holds with one hand things his sister always held with two.

No amount of boy can counteract the sweet, innocent softness of being small and new. He can step on all the bugs he wants, but I know he's scared of dogs and lions and sometimes plays with dolls and always wants his mama when he's had a bad dream. Deep down, I also know he's looking at me and thinking, "She can think I'm as cute and small as she wants, but I can buckle my own goddamn seatbelt, and I've seen tractors and ridden in fire trucks. I have places to go."

Insurance Claim

Ma'am:

We have received your accident-claim reports for the week of June 20, 2010. We regret to inform you that you are ineligible for reimbursement for any portion of the damages incurred to you and your property.

Regarding your personal computer, the homeowners' policy does not cover spills. We are sorry your laptop keyboard "smells like putrid Merlot" and no longer works. While you have provided an affidavit stating that you were not personally responsible for the spill, the person responsible is a minor in your care. Also, your decision to place the Waterford crystal wine glass, filled with wine, next to your laptop qualifies as negligence on your part. This negligence will be reflected in your premium starting July 2010.

Regarding the broken Aqua Globes, the homeowners' policy does not cover frivolous Home Shopping Network purchases or possessions. We are sorry to hear that the same minor in your care "threw them to the ground like Fred Astaire in 'Say It with Firecrackers' while standing barefoot in the driveway." However, if you are incapable of keeping your outdoor plants alive without the aid of an Aqua Globe, we must question your general competence as a caregiver. Your claim has therefore been forwarded to your state branch of child protective services.

Regarding the destruction of your daughter's mobile of the solar system, the homeowners' policy does not cover homemade items, including but not limited to tempura-painted cardboard cutouts cobbled together with kite string. Please give her our condolences.

Regarding the "emotional distress" incurred by you while driving and discovering your automobile instrument panel had been switched to the metric system by the same minor in your care, the automobile policy does not cover ignorance. Pushing the button on your console that says "miles/km" will rectify the situation. Ma'am, it's not rocket science.

Finally, regarding the interior house paint poured on your ceramic tile floor, please refer to the above paragraph referencing spills. The homeowners' policy does not cover them. Any harm caused to the minor during the making of the spill is your sole responsibility.

Ma'am, the nature and frequency of claims you have submitted over the past month make it clear that you have an established history of negligence, putting you in our high-risk bracket. Please be aware that your premium will be raised accordingly starting July 2010, to $2,547.50 per month. We consider this adjustment conservative in light of that destructive little freak you call a son.

Carmen Schofield
USABW Insurance

A Turd in the Tub:

The Magical Thinking of Children

"Mama," he says. "I don't want you to go to jail. I'll miss you." My son pulls me in for a tight hug more suited to the end of a cancer battle than the end of a bedtime.

"Why would I go to jail?" I ask.

"If you broke the blades on the fan," he says, pointing at the perfectly intact ceiling fan above us in his dimly lit bedroom. "Or if you took my favorite drawings and you tore them up, like, a lot."

He releases me as he shoves his quilt and sheets down and tucks his knees into his chest, rolling himself into a ball, trying in vain to aim his butt at the ceiling. In addition to a Pull-Up, he's covered in red flannel, patterned with drawings of Golden Retrievers in Santa hats. He farts and gets back in the covers.

"Then you would go to jail, and then Daddy would have to

48

go see you." His eyes grow wide now. "And then..and THEN…a babysitter would have to come stay with us." So, here we have a scenario in which I go to jail but the agony is all his, because he has to be babysat.

"I'm not ever going to jail," I say.

"Why not?" he asks.

"Because I'm not a bad guy."

My son is four and has just begun to learn—and worry—about bad guys. He asks us often what we would do if a bad guy came into the house. He wants to know where to run, if he should run, what to do if they see him first, and how to know when they're gone. He imagines he's very fast, like a cheetah, fast enough to get to our next-door neighbor's house. He talks about going into the basement, into our tornado shelter, which his mind has distorted into a refuge from any disaster, natural or not.

"Yeah, and you don't wear one of those tall white things on your head," he says.

All I can think of is the Ku Klux Klan. Where the hell has he seen the Ku Klux Klan? I did forget to turn off the TV the day I watched the presidential inauguration. Maybe he saw some archival clip while I was in the bathroom?

"What white thing?" I ask.

"Those things the bad guys wear in that movie. Those white things with the guy who has the mean daddy who breathes like this." He does his best asthmatic impersonation.

"Ohhh, Star Wars!" I say. He's seen only glimpses when his big sister's watching, but apparently the Storm Troopers have stuck with him.

"Yeah, those white things are cold inside, you know." He pulls up his shirt and sticks his finger in his belly button, then puts it in his nose. I don't know if he's transferring lint to nostril or just poking all the holes before bedtime. "Those people, when they get hot, they go inside those suits because it's cold in there."

"So, they're naughty because they're hot?"

"Yeah," he says. And I get the feeling he's trying to work something out. Like why these people are bad. Like why their leader breathes like that. Everything has an explanation. Everything has a reason. Everything has a solution. The magical thinking of children.

"Yup," he says. Then, in usual fashion, he takes one non-sequitur to another. "I'm super strong, though, and you're not. You think you are, but I have two strong things, and you don't have any."

Are we somehow talking about balls here?

My son is at that strange age when his body looks big enough to be logical, but his brain is full of distorted ideas. From believing a mirror won't shatter if it's painted on one side to assuring me that sunglasses will protect people's eyes from the pointy end of a tornado, he's got so much so wrong. Once he asked to tape together two Pull-Ups whose adhesive strips had broken, so he could turn them into "one great big diaper."

In case of emergency, break glass

Sometimes, in my hurried-up, grown-up, critically-thinking mind, I have days where I just can't make sense of him. I'll think we're making headway and then I'll find him trying to use a travel-size Kleenex to clean up a titanic puddle of pee that he somehow misfired onto the bathroom shelf. After our most recent Christmas, he got terribly bent out of shape that I'd tossed our Christmas candy canes—he'd wanted one to put into his cup of cocoa but eventually determined that anything long and skinny would probably be just as good. He started with a sausage stick. Next I found him stirring the cocoa with a raw hot dog. Then a piece of string cheese. "Yuck!" he kept saying. "That's not right either!"

The magical thinking of little kids knows no limits and is a gorgeous thing. Whenever I find myself wondering if my son's got a loose screw, I remind myself that he's just making the world make sense for himself. Don't we all want that? As he grows and gradually awakens to the fact that the world is dangerous, he, like most of us, just needs it to make sense somehow. Bad guys must go bad for a reason. There must be justice for those who do wrong things, whether it's breaking a ceiling fan or breaking into a home. People don't put on full-body plastic armor unless they're hot and the suit's refrigerated.

I often reassure myself with a memory from when I was his age. My sister, six years old at the time, was taking a bath with me. We had a babysitter. I really needed to poop. I'd peed in hundreds of baths with her and never been caught. Why not a turd? Yes, yes, a turd would gently drift out of me and blend in somehow with the bath toys. One minute it was in me, and the next it was gaily bobbing about on the surface like a little skiff. *And I seriously didn't think anyone would notice.* I still remember so vividly how shocked I was when my sister started shrieking, "Jenny pooped in the tub!!!!" I also remember trying to pretend it wasn't mine because I was stealth like that.

If I thought I could drop an invisible deuce at his age, my son is welcome to think tornadoes can poke a person's eye out. I wasn't a toddler. I wasn't a baby. I was four. That is some serious magical thinking.

The Kind of Grandmother I'm Going to Be

First, I might be the kind of grandmother that's coldly called *Grandmother* rather than something endearing like Nana or Grams. I suppose it's possible I could screw things up that much. I hope not, but my children, when they are adults and have become parents themselves, will make the call.

"You know what Mom did yesterday?" my daughter will say. "She left the bathroom door ajar again—knowing, KNOWING that little Zachary [Phoebe, Marjorie, Gabriel, or whatever lovely name my daughter gives her kid] always but always goes in there and eats the toilet paper and splashes in the toilet water!"

"You think that's bad!?" my son will answer. "Last week she let Raphael [Zorba, Puxatawnee, Bethsheba, or whatever crazy thing my son's most assuredly half-cocked future wife names her kid] play with a Tinker Toy in his mouth while he was trying to run!"

They will roll their eyes as they watch me struggle to put diapers on their kids, as I ooze confidence while doing it all wrong, with the adhesive strips on the back sides, pulling it tighter than a Japanese foot-binding, tight enough to cause an umbilical hernia. Behind my back, they will pantomime choking me after I offer their seven-month-olds some grapes or large slices of mango or medallions of undercooked pork and then say, "Oh, should I have cut that up?"

I know I'm going to be that kind of grandmother, because I can't imagine how any sane grandmother can possibly help being otherwise. How can any woman forever hold the dizzying amount of information she learns throughout the course of motherhood—the sort of information that, ironically, we just can't *believe* the generation ahead of us has forgotten or never knew. Like that there's such a thing as baby Orajel, which can be used to comfort teething babies in lieu warm brandy, for God's sake.

I know what kind of grandmother I'm going to be, because I've finally realized not only that I've almost forgotten how to efficiently wipe poop out of the nooks and folds of a walnut-sized vagina but also that I *want* to forget. As soon as my baby son grows out of naps, I'm going to make damn sure I forget what a Halo Sleepsack even is. I'll assume babies can sleep anywhere, even on a pile of industrial work boots if they're tired enough. As soon as my guy can use a regular-size pillow, I'm going to burn from my memory any knowledge of when it's technically safe to introduce any pillow at all. I'll happily forget every goddamned foreboding piece of alarmist advice the American Academy of Pediatrics ever gave. In fact, the kind of grandmother I'm going to be will present to infant grandchildren not just any pillows but perhaps even full-size body pillows. I might let them sleep in a drawer.

Safety? Pshaw! I'll be the kind of grandmother who finds the whole idea of buckling in a car seat for a quick drive as onerous and inconvenient as having to use a belted sanitary napkin. I'll slather any old sunscreen on any age child, maybe even with self-tanner in it by mistake. I'll let them eat cookie dough with raw eggs in it. I'll keep lots of Band-Aids on hand, knowing there will be lots of unnecessary cuts and scrapes on my turf, forgetting about safety gates, assuming babies who can go upstairs can just as easily go down them. I'll give cow's milk to 9-month-olds and allow them to eat dandelions, because dandelions are edible, and by that time, I'll have forgotten about choking hazards. Darn tootin', I will.

Really, we should all have the luxury of one day forgetting all this nonsense we have to learn and allow to dominate our existence for years on end when our kids are wee. Don't you *want* to forget it? Only then can we just be fun and loving, slightly dangerous, supportive but happily deferential—you know, good grandmas who don't actually think they can do better than mama can. Those are the ones who just enjoy the kiddos and try not to break them in the process. Yeah, *that's* the kind of grandmother I'm going to be.

Lessons from Rainman

I have muttered "Rainman" under my breath to my son more than once in his short three years. I've done it about him, to him, at him. In confessing this, I feel like I'm standing in a fellowship hall among strangers and saying, "My name is Jenny, and I'm an alcoholic."

"Rainman" does capture much of what my son does: hyper-fixate, absorb minutiae, repeat himself until I feel like my head might explode. Like my head might explode. Like my head might explode. Like my head might explode. See?

He's painfully literal. Asked if he's cold, he'll feel his skin with his hand before answering, "No, I'm warm." I ask him something simple, and he waits 20 seconds to answer or doesn't answer at all. Passing details can so fully win his attention, so fully fixate him, he's unable to disconnect from them: *That tree's broken? (Yes) It's broken? (Yes) The tree is broken? (Yes) Mama, it's broken? (Yes) Did it break? (Yes) The tree's broken? (Yes).* Is that really any different from *fifteen minutes to Wapner...three minutes to Wapner...one minute to Wapner?*

"He's just a quirky little kid," a neuropsychologist concluded last spring after an hour-long autism evaluation. "He's got a lot of quirks."

"I'm fine with quirky," I said. And I was. I mean, I am.

But sometimes I'm not. I confess I've wondered on occasion if he's somehow broken in a way that will make school, work, or just plain life hard for him. How could I not? Once my dad joked that we need not worry over saving college money for my son like we're doing for my daughter—trade school maybe, but not college. Isn't that terrible? Like father, like daughter: We joke to make ourselves comfortable with what's not.

This is all even worse than it sounds: In my family, questioning someone's intelligence teeters dangerously close to questioning his worth. But I've never questioned my son's worth. There's a delicious beauty in his simplicity, and he's like this fantastic gift that I still can't believe someone gave me. He radiates with a happy-go-lucky spirit, can masterfully handle mechanical things, easily figures out how stuff works, and connects in an intuitive way to music.

But wait. That is a laundry list, now, is it not? Is it some kind of check list I've made to compensate? to defend? Am I just finding ingredients I can use to assemble his beautiful parts into a form that *proves* he's wonderful?

One day I baked cookies while I watched my son playing with an online tangrams program his big sister had left open on our laptop. I was shocked to see him figuring out the puzzles, one after the other, rotating them, flipping them, using the right maneuvers intuitively, piecing the shapes together through level after level. "Wow," I thought. "THERE'S his THING!"

Rolling cookie dough between my palms, I smiled at the back of his head, his little fat toes, his elbows working away at moving the mouse and clicking keys. It's not the first time I've ever felt guilty for the Rainman comments. Why do I ever worry?

After he tired of the game, my son walked partway up our stairs and began calling to me, "Mom, music! Come here!" I followed him and found him on the landing with a little karaoke player his sister recently received for her birthday. Trying to get on his level, I took the mic and began singing something silly. "No," he said with excitement. "MY music. Go to my room. I want MY music." He ran up ahead, and when I caught up, he was already kneeling in front of a CD player there, cueing up the music. "Let's dance!" he said.

For the next 45 minutes, we cut a rug. Now, I have jumped around like a lunatic to many a song with my kids in my life. It's not unusual for me to do the jerk and the monkey and leap off beds in a disco fever. But it's always been kind of a show, a half-assed release that fits within my schedule, my mood, my patience. This time was different.

I'm different, different, different! Nobody is like me! A sort of victory song was the first on the CD, a song by Butterfly Boucher. I was tickled to hear my son sing along: *And that's okay with me! Yeah, that's okay with me!* He was in just his underwear and a shirt, his soft little thighs pumping his body up and down. He was so completely, purely happy. *I'm so tired of being lonely. I still have some love to give.* We danced to the Traveling Wilburys. *And everything feels just as it should. You're part of a life there, part of something good.* We spun to Brandi Carlile. I zeroed in on my son, and all I could think was, "My God, I'm so lucky to be here." I reached my arms up to the air and threw my head back like a holy roller about to speak tongues.

And that's when I felt it.

Childhood. Clean air and brightness. Life running through me, not just my head and not just my heart but all of me. The pure, boundless, lit-up feeling of being a kid. I'd always thought I had a pretty good memory of what it felt like to be young, but clearly I'd forgotten. *This* was age three again, and it wasn't a happy feeling. It was a happy being.

So, guess what? It wasn't those tangrams that mattered. Just like it isn't whether he can figure out any lock or finally say the alphabet. It's about my son knowing the secret to life, like all kids just do, and me having forgotten it. It was a spiritual moment. I can't analyze how. It just was what it was, just like my son is who he is, a thing too free and godly to be measured by words.

When it was time for us to head out for errands, I had a

Rainman moment of my own. I wanted to repeat and repeat and repeat what I'd just felt, spinning with my arms up in the happy light of my beautiful boy and forgetting everything else. Those moments aren't a matter of planning. They're a matter of noticing. Noticing what's right instead of what might be wrong, and truly appreciating it with your whole self. Yeah, my little Rainman can repeat that lesson all he wants. All he wants. *All he wants.*

Super Target Superhero

Who knew how it was going to end up? I had been invited on a last-minute picnic for the first above-60 day since Thanksgiving. Rushing through Super Target, I grabbed so many things, so many attractively displayed $4 things, desperate to fashion our impromptu picnic. We had only 10 minutes. Then we'd be pushing it into preschool time, pushing it into nap time, pushing it into *but-mooooom-you-said-we-were-going-to-a-playground-picnic!* time. So, yes, I speed-shopped the aisle endcaps. I admit it.

It was a shameful display really. Me, I mean. Not the pink-floral melamine bowls or the $5 beach towel, which I flung into the cart like so much pirate booty. And then there was the Pirate Booty itself. And the portable bottle warmer and Gerber puffs and blueberries and bottle nipples. I shoved them all around my kids like they were so many packing peanuts. Truly, it was a shameful display. Me, I mean. Not the miniature bottles of hand sanitizer or the powdered packets of lemonade that practically leapt into my cart in the checkout aisle. We almost had it made. And then it happened.

Drip.

The cashier, God love her, she started a conversation with my preschooler. *How old? When's your birthday? What school? Favorite color?*

Trickle.

Oh, god, lady! The congeniality! The blasted, #$%ing tempo of your bagging as you chat! The time-sucking kindness!

Drop.

How was the cashier to know that I was, at that very moment, experiencing a surge of horrible telltale warmth between my legs? How was she to know that I was lying when I said, "God, it's almost hot today!" as I removed my white (why did it have to be white?) sweater and tied it around the waist of my beige (why did they have to be beige?) pants? How was she to know that, thanks to breastfeeding, it had been more than a year since I had had to gauge and forecast menstrual flow, make decisions about panty liners versus super-plus tampons? How was she to know that my body was suddenly signaling its long-awaited return to fertility? And that the only absorbent

66

thing in my purse was an old Kleenex with crusted child-spit on it?

"Would you like to sign up for a Target Red Card?" she asked.

"No, thank you," I answered. *I've got your Red Card right here, lady! Bag my shit already!*

When she was finally done talking, I raced to the bathrooms, unbuckled my son from the cart, and began Mission Impossible. Yes, I had to put my crawling, mouthing baby on the disgusting bathroom floor. Yes, I had to dig through my daughter's pockets for a quarter while Target-high women walked in and out, wondering why I was shaking down a five-year-old. I suppose they thought I needed one more melamine bowl? Didn't they see the big tampon machine next to us?

I managed to find that quarter. I managed to clean up enough to get out of there without looking like I'd gotten tangled up in a knifing. I even managed my picnic. But as a certain anonymous superhero at the Super Target well knows, I did not manage to remember the red leather purse my parents bought me in Florence, Italy, the one packed with my credit cards, $80 cash, that crusted ball of Kleenex, and no tampons.

When she found the purse hanging on a hook in the bathroom, how could she have known all that led up to it being there? I do not know who she was, only that she turned it in. Today I send a wish out into the universe for her. May she never find herself bleeding down her leg in the Super Target, or anywhere else for that matter.

When Anne Rice Died

We are keepers of chickens, five of them. My daughter and I named them when they began growing their first pin-feathers: Lavender, Gangsta Kathy Jane, Paula Deen, Misha-Rita, and Pip Squeak. A sixth one, Chicken Anne Rice, passed away one spring morning. My then 8-year-old daughter took some measure of comfort in believing Death had been selective and calculating.

"I think I know why *that* one died," she said with knowing and narrowed eyes. She bobbed her head in little damning nods. She'd deduced from the row of vampire paperbacks on our shelf that Anne Rice, whether novelist or hen, was somehow just asking for trouble.

"Shit," I said when I saw the keeled-over hen.

"Shit," said my son, then three years old.

"Don't say that," I told him. "That's a bad word." I opened the coop door and poked a toe at Anne Rice's body. Rigor mortis had had settled in, and she felt heavy. "Shit."

For a minute or so, I entertained the idea of leaving her there so my husband could get her out when he came home that evening. It was a thought I quickly shoved out, knowing it would be a gross display of scream-at-bugs girlishness. I do not like to be thought weak. Besides, the job couldn't wait. At that moment, Anne Rice looked pretty good for being dead: Her eyes hadn't been gobbled, and the other hens had not yet begun to peck away at her "vent"—a place where both poop and eggs exit the body.

"Shit," I said again, and ran inside to grab a few plastic grocery bags.

I kind of forgot for a moment how little my son was, how new he was at this, at seeing death itself. When I came out, he was leaning against the hardware cloth that encloses the coop, the little waffled squares of it making indentations in his soft forehead.

"He died?" he asked.

"Yes, *she's* dead," I answered matter-of-factly. "I have to get her out of the coop."

"Why did he die?"

"*She* died because she must have been very sick." He'd just had a cold, and his eyes flashed at me curiously. His concept of sick wasn't very broad. "But it was a kind of sick that only chickens get," I added.

"What you doing to him?"

"I'm putting *her* in a bag," I said. I pretended this was something I'd done a thousand times. I tried to put on the air of an old farm wife, just going about business in the coop. But it was not something I'd ever done before. I didn't grow up on a farm. I never had chickens. I grew up in a rambling ranch house with a Doxie-Poo named Molly, who died in a vet's office with people who loved her gathered around. And actually, I *was* the girl who ran screaming from bugs.

I pulled a bag back over my hand and arm and tried to grab the bird by her legs. I could feel their texture, cold and reptilian, and I quickly recoiled.

"Is he alive?" my son asked.

"No, *she's* really dead. I just need another bag," I answered as I slipped a second plastic bag on. It didn't do much, doubling up the thin space between my farm-virgin hand and Anne Rice's dead, cold leg. God, she was heavy. It was like picking up a dino-sized drumstick from the Flintstones, but I managed. Quick as I could, I pulled down the edges of the bag from my forearms and over the bird. Then I grabbed a third bag and plopped her in there. Mission accomplished. I'd successfully collected Anne Rice's corpse.

"What you doing with him?" my son asked.

"I'm putting *her* in the garbage," I answered. And I felt terrible. My daughter's first experience with death, well before our son was born, was when our goldfish "mysteriously" died after my husband gave their tank a good cleaning. (*What did you use?* I'd asked. *Bleach* he'd answered.) For her sake, we made a deal of it. We held a backyard funeral, swaddling the fish inside a pretty box. We planted petunias atop their grave. We held hands and said a prayer.

My son's first experience with death? It was watching me shove Anne Rice into a plastic bag and hurl her into our big green city garbage can. Clearly there was a part of me that wanted to be tough in front of him, because even though I say I treat my kids equally, I don't. Sure, I often reassure him that everyone cries. I let him wear pink. I bring him Barbies in the bathtub and tell him I'm happy for him when he announces he's going to marry a little boy we know. But there's this little thing inside of me that I picture as being almost like an owl pellet, a little nugget made up of broken bones and fur and teeth. I notice it only when I'm with my son and only when I face off with "boy moments," like finding dead an animal my husband was eventually going to slaughter anyway. I feel like the pellet was planted in my heart when my son was born, a reminder that there are ingredients to boys that I am sorely lacking. I look at this little brow-furrowed dude with the waffle-weave impression on his forehead, asking death questions with curiosity instead of with sadness, and I try my best to meet him where he's at–sometimes forgetting how very sweet and loving and soft his little heart is.

Sometimes I wish I'd done that day differently. Sometimes I wonder if I did it just right. Sometimes I hope it just blended in with whatever came next. And sometimes I wonder if all he'll remember of it is me saying *shit*. In other words, it was just like every other day since I became a mom.

Head Wide Open:

Screenplay for a Reality Cinema Feature

1st scene, 1st draft

March 2009

1. INSIDE SUBURBAN HOME / DAY

A transitional house positioned drably in the middle of a cookie-cutter neighborhood in Wisconsin. Cold rain falls from a steel-gray sky, ticking away at mashed, yellowed grass in the yard and small clumps of old, dirty snow near the curb. A rickety For Sale sign teeters in the wind, bearing the picture of a slick male realtor on it, and the words "BUY THIS HOME AND I'LL PAY CASH FOR YOURS!"

The house is brightly lit inside, as if to ward off something ominous. Something horrifyingly chirpy plays in the background, Care Bears talking on the TV. The house looks clean, too clean, unusually polished, and something's just not right: There is a crumpled fast-food bag that lists to one side on an overly shiny dining room table. In the sink, next to two empty bottles of wine, are several half-eaten jars of baby food.

Down a short hallway, light shines from a bright yellow bathroom, casting shadows on a rogue pacifier. A small voice becomes audible from within.

CHILD
Ahhhhhhh

WOMAN
What? What's up?

CHILD
It's just, I'm pooping.

WOMAN
Okay. You should probably shut the door.

[Silence as the camera pans the door, catches glimpse of a shadow moving. The door remains open.]

CHILD

It's just that it was *really* big, so it stretched my poop hole really big.

WOMAN [mortified]
Your *what?*

CHILD

My *poop hole*. But it finally came out, and *ahhhhh*.

WOMAN [grunting with laughter]
Um, how big?

CHILD [thoughtfully]
Hmn. It was probably like the size of, like, hmmn, like the fat of your arm kinda fat.

[CUT TO woman's muffin-top spilling over the waist of her jeans as she unzips them and a French fry falls to the spotless couch, sadly.]

WOMAN
Ahhhhh

Fade to black

A Girl and Her Horse

˜

The horses, all three a dusty semisweet rust, didn't belong to us. As far as I knew, they were nobody's, left in a dried-up field where roadrunners roamed and tumbleweeds somersaulted. And the roadrunners and the tumbleweeds roamed and rolled in a fenced-off acreage behind my house so that I felt like the horses and I shared a piece of the earth. In that way, they were mine.

My house was a small cream-and-maroon clapboard, and after I crossed the dirt road behind it, I would have to climb through rusty barbed wire to go any farther. Which I did, and which all the neighborhood kids did, to roam into the calico desert and find horny toads and, once, a sun-bleached centerfold from a pornographic magazine. The Arizona sun was destroying the nude, starting at the staples and working its way out to her thighs. But she was of little interest to me. I was five and had seen girl parts all my life, plenty. But horses? They were dazzling.

When we visited the horses beyond the barbed wire, my

mom brought big carrots, the store-bought kind with no tails. We had to hold them in our splayed palms as the horses approached the last bite, their lips working around their teeth with the dexterity of tongues. The hot air from their noses inking out over my palm scared and excited me. Sometimes my mom would take my palm and set it on the slope between the nostrils, and the horse would look at me with something like recognition. I could see my reflection in its eyes, like looking at a Christmas ball, and the reflections of my mom and my sister and the desert and the wooden stall falling to rot. I really wanted a horse.

When I was several years older, my family vacationed at a dude ranch. At the time, we were living in a new neighborhood where the horses belonged to strangers with upkept fences near trailers on hills. They were *somebody else's horses,* and I could not visit them. For a week straight, by the stench of a hot springs, I rode on a brown horse named Pebbles whose black mane had a cowlick at the withers. We rode every day, up and down steep mountains and through the meadows of rural Colorado. Hot spots formed on the insides of my knees. These turned to blisters. These turned to open wounds. I didn't care. I kept riding.

I always wanted to learn horses, wanted to own one, wanted to go tearing alone through a field on one at a breakneck speed, wanted to know how to care for them in everyday ways. But then there were a lot of things I wanted as a kid – a violin, painting classes, tap shoes—and for my parents, there was no telling whether I meant it. I quit a lot of things that I had begged to have or do.

When I was 30, I took matters into my own hands, as my husband and I took a weekly riding class at Fort Sam Houston in San Antonio. We used *other people's horses,* some of them old and broken in more ways than one, others young and green. They belonged to officers renting stable space. My husband, a sturdy man approaching six feet, was always put on a big, tired, cow of a horse named Sarge. My horse was different each week. The most memorable was a thunderbolt named Charlie.

It was a typical hot day in Texas. I could taste corral dirt gathering in the sweat above my lip. My feet were sweating in my old two-stepping boots, a pointy burgundy alligator-skin pair with embroidery on the kids. The class of adult students had just saddled up, and we were all being led to a practice ring. At the back of the line, my hips were rolling with Charlie's stride. How I loved that sensation of melting into one with a horse. And then, without warning, I was clinging with my knees to 1,000 pounds of meat on a frantic sprint toward the hills. Charlie was going rogue.

The instructor rounded her own horse out of the line, up the hill, yelling for me to pull the reins, which I was already doing with every ounce of strength I had. She seemed a little frantic as she rode up alongside us and somehow managed to herd Charlie back. I don't even know how she did it, but I do know I spent the rest of the lesson on that shit of a horse, terrified. He kept trying to take the jumps in the ring meant for a much more advanced class of riders. I've never been on a horse since. That was 10 years ago.

Looking back, I must admit the seed of horse-fear had been planted in me long before. When I was in the eighth grade, my friend's big sister was thrown from a horse while riding with a toddler. She did not brace her fall or cover her head, choosing instead to protect the child in an embrace. She didn't die right away. She lingered. I still remember the story of her speaking to the nurses after many days of unresponsiveness. "Stop!" she'd yelled. "You're hurting me!" I'm told that was the last time she spoke. I've always wondered if she was speaking to the nurses or the horse.

Now my 6-year-old daughter loves horses. She wants to read about them. She wants to ride our bikes up the road and—oh, how life circles back – feed carrots to *someone else's horses*. One's blind. The other has laminitis, his hoof damaged from too much sugar in the diet. The third is mean and ornery, the Archie Bunker of the bunch. My toddler covers his eyes with his little fists and shivers in my arms at the sight of them all. My daughter looks at her reflection in the sick one's eyes and says, "I want this one."

The funny thing is, I really want her to keep wanting it. I want her to take lessons and know what it feels like to flow with a horse, to move in synchronicity with its body, to know about the quiet and sea-deep bond between a girl and her horse. But she also wants a violin and painting classes and tap shoes. Like her mom, she wants more than she can handle and quits a lot of things she has asked to have or do.

Well, I choose the horses. I choose *for* her. Over the strings and the paintbrushes and the tap shoes, the horses win, because I say so. I make her go to the lessons even when she'd rather stay home. Not so subtly, I pour into her soul a dream of mine that I let die a decade ago.

Don't judge me. I offer to you: Sometimes kids learn to love things because we don't let them abandon pursuit. And sometimes what we don't want them to quit are just the dreams we quit when we had the fickle mind of a child. We see them dip their toe into the water—maybe it will feel good—and we quick punch fickleness in the throat and hide their clothes so that they have to immerse. We make the passion stick this time, hell or high water, because we know they will be rewarded. Not us, them. We spare them from skimming surfaces and missing out on the depths.

As I watch my 6-year-old child walking out a barn door into the backlight of a Wisconsin country paddock, her worn boots dragging on dusty concrete, I wonder how to find the line: Is there really such a difference between imposing upon our kids the dreams we regret not following, as opposed to plucking from their constant river of dreams the few that best dovetail with our own? It's not always bad to realize your dreams through your kids, to let them inherit your passions but not your regrets.

I fear horses, but I love them, too. My daughter has so

much love for horses and just a little healthy fear. This time, whether it was inherited from me or she found it on her own, I hope the love will prevail. I choose to hide her clothes while she tests this water. There's just something divine about a girl and her horse.

Waterboarding

Many moons ago, circa 4 B.C. (Before Children), my husband was in South Korea for annual training with the National Guard. He returned with this handsome pair of newlywed ducks as a gift to me:

Korean Wedding Ducks

Korean Wedding Ducks are meant to be placed in a married couple's home and positioned to indicate the current climate in said couple's relationship. If the birds are touching noses, everything's copacetic. If they're touching bums, there's probably been a tiff. The ducks are super-handy if you're passive-aggressive and need to send a subtle message to your spouse. Not that I would ever do that:

Okay, fine. That's my duck on the left.

To be honest, I altered these ducks right after I got them. True Korean Wedding Ducks come with a ribbon tied around one OR both of their beaks. (Note that I didn't know that there was an option between "one or both" until I Googled *Korean Wedding Ducks* and saw that *most* have both ducks ribbon-gagged.)

This is how they were originally presented to me. Turns out, I am not the only passive-aggressive person in this marriage.

I've had a lot of fun with these ducks over the past decade-plus. Sometimes I'll turn my duck's butt right into my husband's duck's face right in front of him, then walk out of the room. Example? When he ordered a pizza last year on Mother's Day and ate all of it with the kids while I was out delivering a gift to my own mom. He also left me the dishes. *Full disclosure: This is NOT normal behavior for him. He's usually quite thoughtful.*

Still, we've had these ducks for so long, I often forget to use them. In fact, over time, they've migrated from the mantle in our living room to a ledge in our bedroom. This means that if you find a duck with its ass in your duck's face, you're usually unsure about how long it's been that way. It's kind of an unsteadying feeling. You start replaying the past several days—or weeks—to remember what you might have done wrong.

Recently I brought the ducks out of retirement. You see, my husband tends to have a little trouble finding the opening of the laundry hamper. He finds the hamper itself, but it's apparently terribly exhausting to put his clothes all the way inside, like this:

Close but no cigar

I felt that this problem needed some attention. My husband has perfect vision and decent hand-eye coordination, giving me absolute justification in being mad. That is why I summoned the help of the ducks, and they have never been so explicit in their tone. I'm pretty sure he got the message:

Waterboarding

Shoe Shopping:

Fun with Sensory Integration Disorder!

The first pair is too big. It slides off the heel.

The second one is too tight. Just around the pinky toe. She says it makes it fold under.

The third one is too narrow. It causes her bones to feel somehow bonier. What?

The fourth one is also too narrow. You know, like a million rubber bands around her toes?

The fifth one she can't scratch her toes in. It's too smooth.

The sixth one is not good for toe-scratching either.

Nor is the seventh or eighth. She puts them on and twists up her face like a vegan eating whale fat.

The ninth pair leaves room for itchy toes but slides off the heel.

The tenth pair makes it impossible for her to curl up her toes. Deal-breaker.

"Where does it itch?"

"On my toes."

"On your toes. Okay, where on your toes?"

"Under my toenails."

"Under them?"

"Under them."

"Explain."

"Well, I have to have something hard underneath so I can push my toes down on them to scratch under my toenails."

"So, you're telling me you need your shoes to have a harder bottom?"

"No. I need to curl my toes."

"Well, I can think of a few things that would curl your toes."

The eleventh pair gets shoved back into the box really hard after it causes the punched-gut expression. Basically I rape the shoebox with the shoe.

After the twelfth pair, I wonder if the laces would support the weight of my body were I to rip them from the shoes and fashion a noose.

Rejection of the thirteenth pair infuses me with Herculean strength. I'm prepared to pick up the whole goddamn shelf and use it as a shoehorn.

There is no fourteenth pair. No fourteenth!

I stack up the thirteen boxes, a monument to my kid's extra-wide, extra-expensive feet, and I breathe heavy like a moose. We head toward the door, where a woman on oxygen cuts us off at the entry. She's frail, struggling along with her No Country for Old Men tank. She makes her way between us and the door like a turtle on Xanax, and I'm beside myself with wanting to push her down.

Wanting to push down a skinny old lady on oxygen!

I can only thank the baby Jesus there wasn't a fourteenth pair. Number fourteen would have pushed me over the edge. Lord, I came close today. Lord, I came close.

Suck It, Twiggy

"It's unfortunate what we find pleasing to the touch and pleasing to the eye is seldom the same."
- Fabienne, from Pulp Fiction

I keep bumping into Jillian Michaels. Shopping for a yoga video in Target, I'm confronted by her snarling, wolfish beauty on the front of a series of workout DVDs. Rounding into a checkout line with my overstuffed grocery cart, I see her smiling at me from a cover of *Ladies Home Journal*—quietly judging me?—in her workout tank and Spandex pants. Her tiny belly button looks like a typesetter must have misplaced a period, let it slip onto her gut. Dare I call that thing a gut? I guess so, if she's going to keep referring to my flabby butt as glutes.

Like a lot of middle-aged moms, I do not have glutes. I have buns. They are fleshy and dimpled and not at all how I'd like them to be. You could project little films on the breadth of them, but everyone in the films would appear to have the complexion of Edward James Olmos. For years, I've been committing myself to one day fixing these buns. I've dreamt of reclaiming my former body: the 20-year-old thighs that could wear biker shorts (hey, they were cool back then), the 16-year-old calves that propelled me over hurdles like a gazelle. I've not been wimping out on my dream; I've just been having babies. I wanted to finish having babies before undertaking the work.

So, here I am. I'm done having babies, and I've begun my work in earnest. I've lost all the pregnancy pounds and am back to the size I wore when I first met my husband. My clothes fit okay. I don't even feel like beating the crap out of someone every time I try to zip up my pants anymore. I should be content. Instead, I'm rediscovering how much I didn't love my body even before I had kids.

Who knows what you're picturing, but let me tell you I'm a perfectly convenient size and weight. Nobody of my size and weight should be complaining about her size or weight. It could get her jumped and rolled by the truly obese. It's just that I keep bumping into Jillian Michaels. All that taut muscle, those guns she calls arms, legs that look carved and smoothed out of clay: It pains me. I believe my legs look more like gyro-stand gyro meat.

©senkaya - Fotolia.com

To be fair, it's not just Jillian. My real problem is the ideal that's gotten ingrained in my brain. I started thinking about it when I last tried on a swimsuit in front of the mirror, bemoaning not my size but my texture. I'm sort of soft and jiggly. There I stood, holding up my rump with both hands, trying to put the real estate back from whence it came. I was sucking in my gut, imagining what it would be like to have muscular definition leading down into my bikini bottoms like a letter V. And I started wondering why I like how that looks. When did this whole hard-body business for women begin?

I decided to broach the subject with my husband. I couldn't imagine he'd want to wrap his hands around my waist and feel a six-pack. Truly, I doubted he'd prefer the feel of a bowling ball when sliding a hand over my backside. There'd be nothing to squeeze. I wouldn't be soft anymore. I'd feel like a man. Wouldn't I?

Together we reminisced about the ideal women's bodies from decades gone by: from the buxom curves of Marilyn Monroe, to the frail angularity of Twiggy, to the smooth but un-muscular body of Farrah Fawcett. None of these icons were overweight by any stretch of the imagination, but their bodies were so different from each other's. I couldn't think of a one who was muscular and toned the way Jillian Michaels and so many other female body icons are today.

"Do you like that kind of body?" I asked my husband. "Have you, too, gotten used to thinking that looks good?" As I suspected, he confessed to liking a little tone but not nearly as much as all that. And he confessed to preferring a little, oh, how shall I say? Junk in the trunk?

"I don't want to feel like I'm touching a man," he said. Indeed.

Then, strangely enough, I stumbled across a recent study showing that the erotic centers in men's brains are stimulated more when shown pictures of curvy, rounder, J.Lo-butted women as opposed to little skinny Gwyneth Paltrow types. Lithe muscularity didn't cut it for them the way good old-fashioned jiggles and junk do. Strangely enough, men (like women) don't even seem to realize that the new ideal of lean, mean, fighting machine-ettes isn't really their ideal at all.

All of this does little to retire breast augmentations and butt implants, but the study did confirm what I wanted to know: I should quit aspiring to looking like an ice sculpture. My husband kind of likes my gyro legs, as men are wont to do.

Dear Good Samaritan

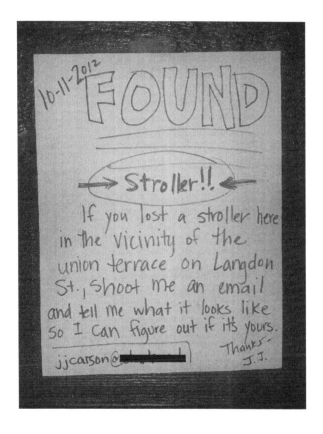

Thanks so much for picking up my stroller yesterday on campus! I know you said you needed a description, so you could make sure it's mine. Well, here goes:

In the back pocket of the stroller, you'll find a Huggies brand diaper bunched into a tight ball full of (now day-old) poop with some gnawed-off, partially digested strands of my favorite blue cashmere scarf in it.

Right around the metal hinges on the left side of the stroller, you will find some taupe-colored stalactites. These are throw-up chunks from yesterday morning. If it would make you feel better, I can bring the new sweater I was wearing, so that you can verify the chunks on its sleeve match up with the stalactites on the stroller.

On the right hinges of the stroller, you will find some avocado. Yes, that is avocado. It turns black after several ~~weeks~~ hours.

I bought some Humphrey's Teething Tablets and Motrin yesterday, and these should be on the seat under my son's speckled blue security blanket. If you look closely, you'll see that the speckles are actually small boogers. Yes, *all* boogers. (He is bonded with them and yesterday marked the 27th day he refused to let me launder the blanket.)

There is a hidden compartment under the seat of the stroller. In it you'll find a baggy of Xanax. If you feel the need to verify that the pills now in your possession are indeed Xanax, I'd be happy to stop by around 8:30 tonight with my 18-month-old. After he pees in your floor vents, topples your CD tower, draws on your walls, and then screams in a Mariah Carey octave outside the bathroom door while you're trying to quickly empty your bowels, you should feel the urge to palm his head like a basketball and hurl him into the next solar system. This is the time to try the pills. Once you're calm, you'll know they were indeed my Xanax.

Finally, if you look behind the headrest, you will find a couple of tampons taped to the canvas. Feel free to toss these out, as I scheduled myself for a hysterectomy immediately after our three-mile walk home yesterday in the drizzle without a stroller.

Thanks for everything,

Grateful Mother

Parenthood:

Where Dreamers Get Schooled

"Mom," my 4-year-old says to me, putting his starfish hand to my lips. "Stop it."

I'm one bar into a lullaby my mom used to sing to me, and he wants me to shut up. I try this exercise every few months, just to see if anything's changed. It's the same lullaby my grandma used to sing to my mom. Actually, my grandma often sang it to me, too. I'd be curled up like a potato bug in a Murphy bed that pulled out of her attic-bedroom wall, and she'd scratch my back with her pearlescent pink fingernails while singing:

Little Indian baby
Hanging in a tree
Don't you wish that you could
Have a crib like me?
And a nice white mama
To tuck you in at night?

And kiss you off to dreamland
Before she takes the light?

Little pale-faced maiden,
With your curly head,
No, I think I'd rather
Have my trundle bed
And a nice brown mama
To tuck me in a tree.
You see, I'm very happy
Because she just loves me.

Yeah, yeah, I know. Like Girl Scout Samoas and the Miami Redskins, my family's lullaby has the political correctness of a bygone generation. Frankly, I don't care; my sentimentality for the song is too strong. I remember with great clarity the comfort of being curled in a blanket and rocked at night in a big mustard-yellow rocking chair as my mom sang it to me. Besides, the PC revision would be even worse:

Little First Nations baby,
In an Amby bed,
Don't you wish that you could
Have an Arm's Reach bed?

My Caucasian mama,
Won't get me one for night
But flips me on my belly
Before she takes the light.

Little settlers' descendent,
The back of your head so flat,
I'm pretty sure I'm okay
Unless sleeping with the cat.
The papoose has been retired,
So my head is nice and round
So, you see I'm very happy,
With the coolest mom in town.

"Why don't you ever want me to sing to you?" I ask my son. I softly brush my fingertips over his closed eyelids. What I wouldn't give to pass down the tradition of singing my child to sleep.

"Because your voice doesn't sound very nice," he tells me. "You have a really, really bad voice."

Hater. Judgy Pants. I'm not *that* bad. And frankly, I'm disappointed. For one, he's crushing one of my *very* few mom fantasies. And two, this is a kid that LOVES music in all its incarnations—except the kind my pie-hole emits.

His big sister used to indulge me somewhat. For years, she'd let me sing not only *Little Indian Baby* but also *The Rainbow Connection* as part of her bedtime routine. But she NEVER fell asleep while I sang—not even once—so my dream wasn't quite fulfilled. I know now she was mostly just trying to prolong bedtime. I had a lot riding on her brother in this department.

The thing is, my son has turned out to be the far more forthright of my two kids. He has told me my butt is bumpy, my hair looks like a witch's, and that my breath smells like poop in the morning. (He's right, on all three counts.) It's never mean-spirited, just telling it like it is. I realize most young kids are unapologetic critics, but he raises it to an art. He's certainly far more candid than his sister ever was.

You know what I wouldn't give to lull my son to sleep with a politically incorrect song my grandma and mom used to sing to me? I'll tell you what: His honesty. It burns me sometimes, but my god, a dream of singing a kid to sleep is such small potatoes—ridiculously small and stupid potatoes. (And what middle-aged woman doesn't want someone who will tell her the truth when she asks, "Do these jeans make me look fat?")

All moms have dreams that get crushed by their kids—whether it's breastfeeding, natural childbirth, or something far more significant. Sometimes what you get in place of the dream is kind of lovely if you just take a step back to appreciate it.

Minutes for July 30, 2010 Family Meeting

Board Members

Present: Chief Executive Officer Mom and Chief Financial Officer Dad

Absent: Ernest and Julio Gallo

Quorum present? No. Not required by benevolent dictatorships.

Others Present:

Kid #1: 6-Year-Old ("Girl")

Kid #2: Toddler ("Boy")

Proceedings:

Meeting called to order at 6:40 a.m. by Boy kicking wall between crib slats, dragging empty cup back and forth across crib railing and yelling for CFO.

Chief Executive's Report:

- After a review by an independent consultant, Michael P. (age 5), it was determined that the family headquarters "always smells weird." CEO recommends that 6-year-old Diaper Dekor be moved to the exterior of the corporate headquarters or at least 50 yards from the executive offices. Discussion was not completed due to entire roll of toilet paper being put in toilet by Boy.

- Staff member, Girl, gave an extemporaneous ~~interpretive dance~~ report on her recent attendance to vacation Bible school. Sign language for *Jesus, hope,* and *baobab tree* were roughly demonstrated repeatedly. It was unclear why *baobab tree* was included, but no further reporting was requested by executive officers. It was requested by the CEO that Girl abandon talks with independent consultant and fellow Bible school attendee, Michael P. (age 5), about her upcoming plans to skinny-dip with Grandma.

- CEO asserts that toilet training negotiations should be abandoned until Boy proves expressive capability sufficient to answer questions about, e.g., the whereabouts of his missing diaper concurrent with his anal sphincter appearing brown.

- CEO mentioned that affiliate member, Grandma, had requested an overnight visit from Boy. MOTION to administer Boy with a spinal block for the purpose of this visit and the preservation of Grandma's 3,178 breakable possessions; seconded but denied.

Finance Committee report provided by CFO Dad

- CFO Dad explained that he had reviewed the organization's bookkeeping procedures maintained by CEO Mom, and found them to be unsatisfactory. MOTION by CEO to cut off CFO's ball sack; no second; motion denied.

- CFO reviewed highlights, trends, and issues from the balance sheet, income statement, and cash flow statement. It was suggested that the CEO review the policies and procedures regarding, specifically, superfluous purchases at Super Target. It was noted by CEO that 90 percent of all purchases made at Super Target worldwide are superfluous. "So, there."

- CFO submitted report of damages and losses for the day prior, due to surveillance, exploration, and construction efforts made by Boy. These include two broken refrigerator locks, dismantled plastic molding around driver's-side seat in company vehicle, peanut butter smears on two sofas, pee on living room carpet, car keys thrown into fish pond, approximately one pound of cherry tomatoes plucked from garden before ripening, approximately 15% of cotton batting (stuffing) removed from small hole made in car seat, loss of fly swatter, bottom portion of dishwasher facing unhinged, bubble machine broken, batteries removed and lost from two remote controls, control knob of CD player broken, ball cap thrown into garbage, spaghetti sauce staining on ceiling above high chair, and approximately one dozen divots in wood cocktail table. CFO proposed that replacements and repairs be delayed until Boy and Girl have been relocated to private offices in remote locations yet to be determined. Discussion tabled due to Boy trying to fill potty seat with water from fridge spout.

· *Development Committee's report* provided by CEO:

- CEO reminded the Board of the impending start of the new school year, and provided a draft schedule of YMCA courses, Girl Scout meetings, library reading hours, and toddler programming available within a 30-mile radius, as well as new vintages of wine due to be released during the calendar year. MOTION by Girl that CEO *formally* abandon own social life; motion tabled due to Boy trying to put goldfish crackers in his butt crack.

· *Other business:*

- Girl requested that CEO abstain from exercising authority over television viewing programs and times. CEO proposed that all household TVs be donated to the needy. Discussion tabled due to general staff hysteria.

- Boy commented, "Blerg, grro, beeboww, ffff, digger." Noted.

· Meeting adjourned at 7:30 p.m. due to engorged forehead veins as well as corporate bedtime procedures.

· Imbibing commenced at 7:33 p.m.

· Minutes submitted by CEO

9/11

This morning as I sat in church with my 6-year-old daughter, watching her wipe a booger in the church bulletin again, I thought of something that made my stomach lurch: I almost didn't have her. In fact, I almost didn't have any kids at all.

I was nowhere near the terrorist attacks when they occurred. I was living in San Antonio. Yet, like most everyone I know, I was undone that day in a fundamental and irreversible way. My body ached from the sad. I cried in my bed at night, afraid of the world outside my door. I could not shake the images of people in business suits leaping from burning skyscraper windows, an act of horrible fear and courage all wrapped into one. I kept imagining what they'd been doing just moments earlier, and the terror they had to have felt just before they died. I listened to broadcasted recordings of goodbyes left on answering machines, and I cried over those lives. But I cried too over the lives I was no longer planning to bring into this world. Suddenly the world seemed too scary a place to raise kids.

Obviously, I went on to have kids. But I also went on to experience two big personal losses to 9/11. Years after the attacks, my husband deployed to the Middle East for 15 months with the National Guard, when our daughter was just a toddler. While he was gone, one of our friends was killed by a suicide bomber in Afghanistan. So indeed, my dread on 9/11 did prove to be grounded in some way. But the world wasn't changed in quite the ways I'd imagined it would be. It was the frog coming to a slow boil in a pot, heating up so gradually that the temperature doesn't seem so bad. I've grown accustomed to a higher temp.

Now I can't remember quite what life felt like before 9/11. On the surface, it looks so much the same: I still see kids swinging on tire-swings in their yards. Crossing guards still wave and smile. We go to the movies. I worry about my jean size. The bills arrive. The junk mail comes. We rake leaves and shovel snow and plant gardens. We go to the dentist and the doctor. We barbecue and bake and pickle our cucumbers. And we raise our kids and, some of us, spend time at our little laptops writing about them.

But when I stop to consider it, as I do every 9/11, I am sure the world is a very changed thing indeed. I mourn that change in a less acute, less concentrated way than I mourned lives on the day of the attacks, but mourn it I do. Today as I watched my daughter wiping her little booger on the damn church bulletin in her lap, instead of admonishing her, I noticed her—*really, really* noticed her in a way that caught my heart in my throat. I let my eyes scan over her fluffy tulle dress, her little red shoes, the lip gloss gripped in her sticky fingers, all those freckles, her tangled hair—and I realized that I almost let terrorists take her from me. I almost let them take my child.

I will always mourn the reality taken from me by September 11. But I'm thankful that the fear gave way to more important things. I'm thankful that, eventually, love prevails. Love always prevails.

Dear Management

I am writing to request an opportunity to meet with you to review my position with this firm. I feel the timing is appropriate, because I have been at this job for five years without a promotion. To boot, I have been working *pro bono*.

I received my current position based, apparently, on the seven babysitting nights I had between the years of 1984 and 1989, one of which included me surviving a stabbing in the arm with a sharpened pencil wielded by a psychotic two-year-old. Between that and my own personal desire to bear children, I believed I could do this job. Apparently, you did, too. Thank you for your trust.

Since taking the job, I feel I've more than proven myself. Excepting the Great Ancora Coffee Shop Episode of January 2009, I have successfully taken responsibility for all bodily fluids released from all orifices of two small human beings. In the course of my work, I have sewn miniature ball gowns from swimsuit fabric. I have eaten cheese-filled hotdogs. I have refrained from gagging while cleaning up stew barf. I have sewn drapes. I have wiped, scrubbed, sniffed, and dug out from under my fingernails all manner of defacatory substances. I have clarified grave confusion on a wide range of topics, from labia to secondary colors to death. I have used my breasts and body to triple the size of two small human beings. My knowledge and skill in the Imaginative Arts is unparalleled, as evidenced by the 673 (and counting) original stories I have told, including today's installment in the Koka and Goldsash series featuring two fist-sized kittens. Sir, my God, *I have played My Little Pony.*

I have demonstrated an ability to work independently and take initiative. (I refer you to the 15 months I spent as a single parent while my husband was deployed, as well as the offer I made yesterday to make a crafting afternoon out of white tennis shoes, a glue gun, small gems, and glitter glue.) I regularly put in long days, weekend work, and "on-call" work.

My commitment to this job is obvious, as evidenced by the 85-minute bedtime fiasco I championed last night as well as by this morning's episode involving my spitter-upper being allowed to bite my tongue after eating. (Everything into the mouth, right?) I would like you to know that I view my future as a mom very positively. I want to continue to make noodle necklaces. I anticipate someday having an entire noodle jewelry line. My relationship with boogers remains in the developmental phase, but I assure you, is not being neglected.

I am confident that you will sincerely consider my request for a promotion. Based on the birth of my second child seven months ago, I have been led to believe that you are satisfied with my work. Wait, was *that* the promotion? *Mother of Two?* If so, might I suggest you carrot me along with a more systematic reward system, perhaps using badges (e.g., a Master of Colic badge) or a bit of flair (e.g., an "I Survived Projectile Diarrhea!" button)?

I look forward to hearing from you very soon.

Sincerely,
Mom

End of Days

I have menorrhagia, which I believe is Latin for scenes from the Colosseum. Days 1 and 2 of my period are a laborious affair, involving frequent trips to the bathroom and all sorts of backups to my backups to my backups. Kotex executives should thank their lucky stars for me, because I believe my period is what funds all their summer homes. I didn't really think it could get any worse, but then I had a son.

It was a gorgeous sunny April morn, marred only by water bloat and bad skin. My 18-month-old and I were heading out the door when my feminine-protection levy threatened to break. As usual, the threat was sudden, drastic, requiring catlike reflexes. I ran back to the bathroom, carting my son on my waterlogged hip, and set him on our bathroom floor as I tried to rush through the procedure. (With menorrhagia, it can be referred to as a *procedure*). He had never witnessed this act, thank God. And I trusted he'd be preoccupied enough with the shower door to stay oblivious to my handiwork. But between the toilet bowl under me, the toilet paper un-twirling next to me, and the string dangling from beneath me, I could not have been more wrong.

The problem was that I felt rushed. I didn't want my son intensely studying me just then, the way he often does. In my panic of trying to change the tampon by sleight-of-hand, I got butterfingers. The whole thing swan-dived into the toilet: not the new tampon, mind you, but the old one — and not in clean toilet water but in freshly minted pee-filled sewage.

I took three horrified seconds to decide that I probably couldn't flush the thing down our 1985 pink porcelain POS, so inhaling bravely, I ripped a hunk of toilet paper and went fishing. Success! Or was it? My weak grip dropped the "fish" back into the bowl, sending pink splatters onto the toilet seat. What could I do but bare-hand the thing out of the bowl? A sudden onset of violent dry-heaving made me hasty in my aim toward the trash. Which is to say I ended up with splatters — oh, God, how it splattered — on the wall and the floor and my face. *Yes, my face.*

And here, of course, is where my darling boy became disinterested in the shower and noticed the toilet bowl was open. As he began to toddle to it, those cute fat thighs crunching his diaper with each horrifying step, I could only waddle frantically toward interception, with my pants around my knees, holding toilet paper to my nether parts, and trying with my free hand to wipe the seat as I yelled NOOOOOoooOOOoo! Shoving him with one foot away from the mess on the floor as I erstwhile wiped streaks off the cabinetry and hoped to God he wouldn't grab the rogue tampon, it seemed to me that I had just learned a very basic lesson about Things Not to Do with Your Baby Boy.

Boys—*all* boys—even the kind prone to pyromania or with soft spots that haven't yet closed– they're all safer on the loose for three minutes than they are trapped in a bathroom with mom during her personal End of Days. In case of emergency, yes, *do* leave your toddler strapped into his seat in the car. *Do* hand him over to strangers in checkout lines. Whatever it takes, ladies. Because once a month, it's okay. Boys don't belong in in the Red Tent.

Hand-Me-Downs

My children wear memories belonging to others. In a cornflower blue dress I bought for my niece eight years ago, my daughter leaps across the lawn. In godawful circa 1980 jammies my friend inherited from a friend from a friend from a friend, my son lays kisses on me in the rocking chair in the dark. We make our own memories in these clothes, but they have other histories.

Twelve years ago, just after I met my husband, his sister had her first child. For years I bought our niece little outfits I loved, never imagining they'd return to me one day when I had my own daughter. They come to me each season, taped in cardboard boxes, smelling of foreign closets and fabric softeners. Many are faded and wrinkled, from being worn while climbing trees or sliding into home bases, or from simply being the favorite. When we come to visit her family, my sister-in-law tilts her head sideways in a bittersweet way and tells me, "That dress! I remember when Shannon used to wear that dress!" And I feel happy, like my children are wearing more than clothes. They are wearing good karma.

It's not just family that hands down our clothes. We recently moved to a new neighborhood, and I've made friends with a woman whose son is a year older than my own. Last month, she began a mother's bittersweet ritual of handing over fibers soaked with her memories, giving her boy's old clothes to my 20-month-old son. When she sees him wearing one of these outfits, she gets a sweet smirk on her face. It's the look of a mother who might want to do it all over again, the look of a mother who doesn't want to do it all *ever again*. (They're the same, in a way.) I can feel the love when she tells me, "I remember those little pants!"

There have been other kids' potty accidents in my kids' clothes. The garments have been snagged on swing seats in playgrounds we've never visited. They've been worn too big and too small, by kids bigger and smaller than my own. Other little butts, now bigger butts, never looked cuter in them at family reunions. Someone else's sweet babies have been nursed in them, rocked in them, and chased and loved in them.

When I rock my son at bedtime, I think of how many memories I hold in my arms, and that some of them aren't even my own. The intensity is strongest when he sports

122

the tackiest, ugliest hand-me-down jammies we own. They're sunflower yellow and bright blue, pilled fleece with an anchor stitched into the thickness of the front. They button up at a diagonal and make him look like a seasick starfish. I love these horrible jammies. They are different from what I see in the stores, so I feel like they are My Son's Jammies. Yet I know they have belonged to many others, and for every memory I've attached to them, there are a dozen more that belong to some other child's mother. I imagine someone's uncle wore these, someone's nephew, someone's child, and they've been handed down and down and down. I know that for decades they've been the canvas of other kids' projectile vomit and more poop leaks than I can shake a stick at. But I will never forget my son in those jammies, and they will always be a part of my happiest of days.

Hand-me-downs are like sourdough starter: You can make something new from them, but their value comes from where they've been, how long they've been going, and how long they'll keep going. Their very fibers are chains of love.

The Naked Truth:

Screenplay for a Reality Cinema Feature*

Opening Sequence/Second Draft

September 2012

SETTING: SUBURBIA / GRAY AUTUMN DAY

Begin with aerial-view extreme long shot that slowly zooms in on 1980s home sandwiched between a Wisconsin suburb and a yellowing cornfield. Gray clouds fill the sky. A single hummingbird feeder hangs from a dead branch. Chickens peck through fallen leaves. Medium shot as a rust-red hen defecates next to a melamine Christmas plate in the river rock around the deck and squawks. Extreme close-up on poop. Brief flashback, long shot handheld, showing young, smiling couple backpacking on a picturesque mountain, their laughter echoing in a green valley below them. Return to extreme close-up of chicken poop.

Canted angle, medium view, hand-held shot of interior of house. The light in the house is the same gray as the light outside. In the background, a Wii game plays a hillbilly theme with banjos and cowbells.

TODDLER [YELLING FROM ANOTHER ROOM]

"Helllp! I do it again!!!!"

Camera alternates close-ups with extreme close-ups, showing Lincoln Logs, a child's fleece pajama top, a Barbie with shorn hair and a missing limb, laundry half-folded in baskets, a piece of sausage on the kitchen tile, and two empty wine glasses next to an empty wine bottle and a spoon in an empty jar of peanut butter. Brief flashback to medium shot of smiling couple lazing on a beach, dog-eared novels on their chests, their laughter competing with the sound of waves crashing. Return to extreme close-up of greasy sausage on tile. Cut to medium shot of toddler seated on carpet, putting a large Lincoln Log on his penis.

TODDLER [quietly singing]

It's on a penis, on a penis, on a penis, on a penis!

Low-angle shots of tops of shelves and bookcases and fridge, showing Nesquick powder, a vacuum food-sealer, a game of Mousetrap, and a splatter of oatmeal on the ceiling. End on extreme close-up of booger on a wall. Cut to shot of man reading to young girl on a couch, naked toddler seated near their feet playing with Lincoln Log.

MAN

"But his eyes were bigger than his stomach. He saw six different cranberries…"

TODDLER [quietly singing]

It's on a penis, it's on a penis, it's on a penis!

Close-up of man's mouth, showing five 'o clock shadow.

MAN [STILL READING]

"Then he saw the gravy, brown and luscious, in a silver gravy boat…"

Sounds of gunfire, camera switches to eye-level medium shot of toddler now playing a Wii video game, shooting virtual tin cans.

MAN [STILL READING]

"Down fell the carrot sticks, still impaled on the olive…"

Cut to medium shot of woman in robe. Zoom to extreme close-up of her mouth, showing her unwaxed upper lip and her jaws working furiously at a mouthful of Goldfish crackers.

WOMAN

I said no more video games!

Medium shot of man with girl, looking up from their book.

MAN

Mom said no more video games.

Man resumes reading. Close-up of girl's face as she listens, her eyes then widening in horror.

GIRL

He's putting a log on his privates!

Extreme close-up of peanut butter in girl's uncombed hair

MAN

Hey, don't put that on your penis!

TODDLER BOY [screaming, wielding Lincoln Log and Wii remote]

More wideo! I want it on a penis! I do it! I DO it!

Medium shot of woman in robe, head resting in hands.

WOMAN

No Lincoln Logs on penises. Logs are not for penises.

Brief flashback to close-up of wood burning in a campfire, pull back to show young couple relaxing in camp chairs, the man holding an acoustic guitar, and the woman holding a novel. They laugh over the sound of a whippoorwill singing in the trees. Cut to naked toddler.

TODDLER BOY [Trying to pull down his pants]

Want to see my seaweed?

Extreme close-up of woman's wedding ring as her hand descends aggressively into a box of Goldfish crackers.

WOMAN

That's not seaweed. That's a penis.

YOUNG GIRL

Don't put logs on the seaweed. Which log touched it!?

Extreme close-up of woman's hand as it plunges farther into the crackers, up to her wrist, giving the appearance of an amputated stump.

Fade to black.

*Script to be possibly repurposed as a condom commercial.

Apology to My 6-Year-Old

Darling,

First, let me start by saying I had no idea that you now require all four edges of your bread crusts to be removed. Though I know you detest eating anything "too brown"—and, by the way, I feel like a jerk for not seeing the nuances of brown you see—I got it in my head that you would use the crusts as a sort of handle and eat around them. I am such an idiot.

Second, please forgive me for asking you to keep your butt on your chair for an entire mealtime. I don't know where I get these ridiculous ideas. I mean, really, who do I think you are? Christopher Reeves? Of *course* you need to get up and dance with a mouthful of potatoes, spraying my plate with little white chunks as you laugh. It really never gets old, no matter how many times you do it. I'm ashamed I ever asked you to stop. Can you forgive me?

Third, it sickens me that I can't stop telling you to clean up after yourself. Really, in a way, can't anything in the world be a garbage can if we decide to make it such? I'm so terrible at this philosophical stuff. I know you're just more evolved than I am. Honey, I'm trying to learn from you.

Fourth, I simply have no excuse for my repeated inane requests that you put on some underwear and quit resting your Netherlands on our furniture. Lord knows a little dingleberry isn't going to hurt anyone. Not that you'd have any. I know what a master of wiping you've become in your four long years of toileting. And it's not like you haven't bathed in the past week or two.

Which reminds me: I'm sorry I keep making you wash yourself. I feel like such a monster. You have *so much* on your plate already—the reading, the swinging, the opening of your new play restaurant. Who needs to wash their crotch on top of all that? As if tree sap on your forehead is going to attract dirt! As if dreadlocks aren't all the rage!

Oh, and if I may say so, this notion I can't seem to shake? That you have to brush your hair every day? It's a relic from my own childhood. You know, I had an abusive mother, too. Does the name Grandma ring a bill? Shudder. I haven't gotten counseling for it yet, which (I'm sure) is why I am projecting this hygiene thing onto you. Your hair really does look smashing when it's all matted up against the side of your head and has a ladybug barrette randomly placed amid the bangs that you like to part in the middle with your fingers. The people seem to love it.

There's so much more, honey. How can I ever ask forgiveness for all my transgressions? Making you wear the same pajamas two nights in a row, offering you that granola bar you loved yesterday but which disgusts you today, reminding you to stop picking your nose, not letting you bike by yourself around the corner where the sex offender lives, and worst of all, not being wildly entertaining and/or a rapt audience during your every waking hour. I'm so sorry, sweetie. I'd much rather have a contented little girl with cavities and dreadlocks *now* than a respectful, responsible, and honorable adult *later*.

Here's to living for today!

Signed,
Your Humble Servant, Mom

Older

"Grandma's such a funny woman, isn't she?" I say.

"She's not a woman," my daughter harumphs. "She's an old lady!"

"Maybe to you," I say. "Why do you think she's old?"

"Because she's all wrinkly," she says.

I pause to look at her smooth, pink skin freckled by six summers. I remember how my grandma looked to me at that age, very pretty but saggy in the face.

"*You're* wrinkly, too," she tells me.

I check to see if she's wearing her teasing eyes, but they aren't there. These are her matter-of-fact ones.

"Maybe to you," I say.

It bothers me that my daughter will never know me as a young woman, a girl with a wild streak, someone who could still turn a back flip at 25. It bothers me that I can't introduce my six-year-old self to her six-year-old self, let them be friends. I think they would be, but that's not really what's eating at me. It's my own mortality, and how much more aware of it I am through my daughter's eyes. Do I really have to leave her someday? Impossible.

The next week we are driving from the hospital, where my dad is in the cardiac unit again. He's recovering as well as can be expected, but the sight of him makes me weak. He's going to need a heart transplant, soon, and the waist at the hourglass of his life feels horrifyingly wide. I feel heavy all over my body, like someone has poured sand in my veins. My daughter had brought to him a drawing of a unicorn, handing it over while eyeballing his IV tubes and the bags and machines hovering around him like soul-sucking ghouls. The sharp angles and bloodlessness of his face when he smiled were almost unbearable. Is he really going to leave me someday? Impossible. Not *my* dad.

On our way home, we pass the cemetery where I'm told comedian Chris Farley is buried. It's catty-corner to a high school, plopped on a sort of island between roads that cross each other at berserk angles chopping the land into pie-pieces. One stretch of the cemetery is basically on a really wide median, separated from the other graves by the road on which my daughter and I are driving. There's just no averting our eyes and pretending we're not driving through a death park. I look in the rearview mirror to see what my daughter's making of all those gravestones, going on and on and on like a threat so thinly disguised as a promise.

"Look at that enormous one," I say. "That's ridiculous, trying to look so important even after you're dead."

"I like the one with the flowers," she says as we pass a grave surrounded by wrought-iron plant hangers with blossoms cascading out of them. "Mom, when I die, what kinds of flowers are you going to bring to my grave?"

Trying not to look sucker-punched, I tell her I'm going to die first, because I'm the mom and she's the kid. That's how it usually goes. Then I ask her what flowers she'll bring to *me*. I don't remember what she says because I'm frightened by all of it. I don't ever want to leave her. In the rearview mirror, I check again, and she looks just fine.

"You know what would be funny?" she says. "If after you died, you came back as a ghost and you lived in our house!"

135

I tell her I don't want to do that, and she furrows her brow and asks why.

"Because I want to go to heaven and get things ready for you there." I feel dirty inside, being so trite.

"Good," she tells me. "We're going to have a lot of fun together in heaven."

My crow-footed eyes narrow at myself in the mirror, and I feel like such a liar: Despite my best efforts, I haven't any real faith that there's a heaven. I tell her I do, but I don't. I have only the hope and inclination to believe there's something after all of this. I've made myself okay with lying about this one thing. Because maybe it's not really a lie. And maybe it's the only way we can drive by cemeteries, looking at the backs of our wrinkled parents' heads leading the way to death in front of us.

Prayer of Thanks for the Childless

HER: "Okay, so you take a piece of medical tape and strap it from one armpit — no, no, wait — one boob part of one armpit. Do you know which part I mean? It's not really your armpit, but it's not totally your boob either."

Dear God, thank you. Thank you for a conversation about something other than tear-free detanglers and how to wipe a wee scrotum covered in poo granules.

ME: "So you go from armpit to armpit with it?"

HER: "Kind of but more like boob to boob, so they're pulled together by this thing, and whammo, you've got cleavage."

Thank you, God. Thank you for a conversation that isn't about arm floaties or whether two is too young for Crocs. I love you, Jesus.

HER: "Is it a strapless dress? How far does the thing plunge? I mean, is it meant to show some cleavage?"

ME: "No, it's sort of 1950s-ish, with tapered straps and a heart-shaped neckline and…"

Holy Spirit, O giver of perspective, I am so building an altar, and you are so having lamb chops tonight.

HER: "I totally know what you mean. If it's thin, you might not want to have your boobs taped, but this is old school, old school, old school — like, women have been doing this forever."

ME: "No, this sounds perfect. Geez, I might just tape them every day from now on."

El Shaddai, praise be for reminding me there's something else women have been doing forever with their breasts other than breastfeeding. I suckle from your holy teat.

ME: "I should tape them together this afternoon and see if the mister notices tonight. Like, I'll just be wearing my old crap clothes but have big cleavage and perky breasts."

HER: "Yeah! You can really make your boobs look pretty big with just a roll of medical tape. You'll look hot."

Lord, thank you for a simple conversation about boobs, just plain boobs, and not lice or molars or potty training or daycare or vaccines or the supposedly-cute-effing-thing that cowlicked so-and-so did at bedtime yet again and again and again. Seriously. Thank you so much for my friends without kids. Amen.

Hands

I thought of you today, when I lifted your brother from a shopping cart. He's beginning to cling back, laying his head sometimes on my chest or shoulder in a way I don't remember you doing. He does many things I don't remember you doing, like working at gears and locks and switches with the dexterity of a mime. You were never good with your hands. It's funny that his little starfish hands reminded me of you.

At his age, your hands were smaller and more delicate, with papery nails I could easily tear when they got too long. Yours never held a bottle. They kneaded against my hair and my belly as you nursed. They waved earlier. They pointed more. "Tzat?" you said as you pointed. "Tzat?" They clenched up for different reasons than his do, into hard little fists the size of new potatoes. When *he* does that, it's frustration; when *you* did that, it was to amuse us with delusions of Herculean strength.

Your bedtime hands are what I remember best. Lying in

bed with you each night when your dad was deployed, feeling so exhausted and ready for the day to end, I loved to drape your palm over my belly. No matter what shenanigans had transpired before those sweet-relief bedtimes, no matter how summer's light coaxed and tickled at the edges of your thick window blinds, no matter how loud the older children laughed and played in the alley outside, you still let me hold your little fingers and sing to you as though I were better than all of it. Your fingers, already years free from my womb, still curled toward your palms the way a newborn's do. After you fell asleep, I would stare at them, trying to memorize their shape. Which I did. I knew, just knew I was going to miss them more than many other things. Which I do.

Yesterday we walked across the road from our backyard to investigate the fruit on a neighbor's tree. Cherries, were they? Crabapples? You wanted me to check. Even though it was the end of a dead-end street, I tried to weave my fingers through your reluctant ones as we stepped onto the asphalt. It was cheating, I admit, using the excuse of traffic safety so that I might hold your hand.

You see, for months now I've been feeling your hand growing out of mine. It's not just the size. It's also the texture. There's this different kind of stickiness, some sort of telltale shift in the recipe of sweat and food and anatomy that makes your hand feel a little clammy, harder, and dirtier. It doesn't hold tightly anymore either, doesn't mindlessly seek mine the way it once did. It's no secret to me: You are growing up.

Know this: It can't be helped that I'll cheat to hold your hand whenever I can, clinging a little to what I once recognized as the exact shape and size and texture of trust and comfort. Your brother's hand cannot replace yours. It's you that I miss. But when you slip your hand out of mine, knowing danger isn't imminent, don't think I don't understand. Even in your little 5 1/2-year-old incarnation, you are discovering your own two legs. It means I am fulfilling my work as a mother.

Abandoning the charade of protecting you from invisible semi-trucks, I let you let go yesterday mid-street. It wasn't because I knew your brother would put his trusting hand in mine soon enough. I just understood you didn't want my protecting lead, and mothers shouldn't cling.

"Sometimes I like to hold your hand just because it feels good to hold hands," I offered. That's the truth, you know?

And you, my sweet love, you caught my hand back up in yours and agreed.

Honey, When I Was Your Age...

I can remember being the age my daughter is now. I don't just remember awful moments of crapping my pants or sitting quietly terrified among cobwebs during hide-and-seek. No, I also remember how good it felt to finally get out of my *Sesame Street* Ernie sheets in the mornings when they were wet with my pee. I remember how my sister's small arm felt around my shoulders for photographs, the only time she put it there. I remember the feel of red Pyracantha berries when I squished them between my fingernails. Yeah, I'm talking details here: I mean I *really* remember being my daughter's age.

My daughter is four-and-a-half, and this is a big milestone year for many reasons other than that she's reached the Age When Long-Term Memory Kicks In. It's kindergarten year, for example. She had a kindergarten sneak-peek and assessment today, getting to spend a couple of hours in an actual classroom with hardened veteran kindergarteners, doing kindergarten things. Honestly, I hadn't much considered the gravity of our future until the grim reaper from the PTA announced to parents in the auditorium that there would be a "Boo-Hoo Breakfast" for us the first morning of real kindergarten — stocked with coffee, muffins, and "lots and lots of Kleenex."

"Will smelling salts and satellite conferencing with Dr. Phil be provided?" is what I thought about saying.

"Can we find out more about working with the PTA?" is what I really said.

"Shit. I am going to cry like a blubbering drunken Real Housewife of the OC," is what I was really thinking.

After her sample class, my daughter and the other newbies got to clamor around in a parked school bus. She asked if I would join her inside, and she led me to the back back, showing me where she would sit.

"Honey, people have laid down their lives to NOT sit in the backs of buses," is what I thought about saying.

"Keep in mind that if you sit in the back of the bus, you have to wait the longest to get off the bus," is what I really said.

"No, child! If you sit in the back of the bus, you might see older boys

showing each other their penises or trying to touch girls' breasts while sexting," is what I was really thinking.

Later, I asked her how she felt about her practice day of kindergarten. She'd had a handful of craft projects, a nametag hanging cockeyed off her coat, and a loosed ribbon on her ponytail. It looked as though someone had tried to cram a year's worth of *kinder-wunder* into her with a mallet. She was breathlessly delighted, but true to form, she highlighted the lowlights for me: She'd had to sit next to an assigned buddy during snack time, and not the "pretty, pretty girl with the long hair," which apparently mattered a whole lot.

"Honey, the pretty, pretty girl with the long hair is rarely really nice in elementary school," is what I thought about saying.

"You know, you can't tell how nice people are by looking at them," is what I really said.

"Hello? That girl boasts the best odds of making you feel like a failure for wearing stripy socks instead of High School Musical socks and not owning an American Girl doll," is what I was really thinking.

146

On the way home, I stopped at the corner where her bus stop will be. One of the intersecting roads is pretty speedy. I noted this in the same place in my brain that earlier noted the pickup time would be 6:57 a.m. — for an 8:10 school start time. I never intended for her to take the bus at all, but it's clearly something she wants to try. I'm attempting to give the idea some real consideration, but come on.

"Just think about sitting on a bus feeling motion sickness for two hours every day!" is what I thought about saying.

"Honey, we'll probably park over here and wait in the car each morning, to keep out of the cold and traffic," is what I really said.

"Listen, my first day at a bus stop, I asked Shelly Mann what time it was, and she said, 'Half-past a monkey's ass, quarter to his balls,' and I almost cried when I had to get on the bus with her, and I just want you to stay inside a bubble a while longer, and don't you, too?" is what I was really thinking.

You think your childhood memories are going to serve you well as a mom. You think they'll help you bring such empathy and compassion and wisdom to the table. Sometimes they do. But sometimes? They just make you a nut-job.

Jack Frost Nipping at Your Soul

Winter's coming. I can feel it in my bones and see it out my window. Another mom told me yesterday that her Volvo even warned her about it.

"The little frost symbol came up on the display," she said.

The Volvo is certainly onto something.

Wisconsin makes me blue this time of year. I want to appreciate the turning, falling leaves, but all I see are tree branches scribbled up in dead gray tangles against a white sky. I want to enjoy the brisk morning air on my cheeks as I open the door to check what the kids should be wearing. Instead I shiver and think to myself, "It's too soon." Summers come and goes by so quickly. Springs and autumns happen in a blink. Winters wear on and on and on. The thought of facing another one makes me want to curl up in a fetal position.

I am raising Wisconsin kids, though, and reading the *Little House* books while I do it. My own little modern-day Laura

Ingalls looks out the windows each morning and tells me she misses snow. She can't wait to jump into it, eat it, and dress for it. She prefers icicles to ice cream. My baby boy has already begun to show a disinclination to blankets and warmth, too, just like his sister did as a toddler. I wonder if either of them will own a hockey stick or learn to ice fish. It's all so different from my Arizona childhood, when school could be called off over the sight of one's own breath condensing in the air.

I'm trying to learn from my kids, to catch whatever it is they've caught. I want to face the autumn with joyous expectancy rather than a heavy heart. I want each red leaf that falls on my car's windshield to remind me of life, of jumping headlong into a leaf pile, rather than death and wanting to jump headlong off a bridge. Bundling up, sitting by a fireside, eating warm grilled cheese sandwiches with tomato soup, and drinking hot cocoa with little marshmallows in it. Walking in the eerie hush of new snow at night. These are things I must remember to appreciate. These are things I believe my kids are slowly teaching me to value. Kids teach us a truckload about just living.

Last night we knelt at my daughter's bedside and said a prayer. I asked God's help for those in pain, those who are tired, and those who are lonely. When I do that, I'm usually thinking of Everyman, of faceless people in faraway places. This night I realized that there are a lot of people in my life right now who are in pain, tired, or lonely: My friend whose soldier husband is deployed. My friend whose mariner husband has been gone too long. My pregnant friend who's been evicted. My many friends struggling with depression. My sister, who's going through job stress. My dad, whose heart is failing. Me. So many of us are already deep in a sort of winter of the soul, and now we must face together the literal long, long winter ahead. How can we do it?

I cannot help but think about Caroline "Ma" Ingalls and wonder if she made it through these winters partly because she had little ones outside her door making snow angels and begging for molasses candy trickled and hardened on snow. We parents are blessed to be led through the seasons by our kids. Not just the literal winters but the dark, cold winters of the soul.

This morning I rolled out of bed and felt like I'd been crying in my sleep. My chest was so heavy, and it got heavier when I looked out the windows to the west and saw gray clouds hanging there. But when my daughter ran into the room, she was fully clothed in a sweater dress and warm tights, bright colors that lit up the room. When we raised the blinds on the windows to the east, we were surprised with a beautiful purple-pink sunrise.

"It's a lucky day!" she said. "Those are my favorite colors!" Her warm words steamed up the window, so I reached out and traced a heart there with my finger. And I felt just then as though God, whoever and however and wherever, must have heard my prayer. My child was his reply.

Dear Director of Public Works

Please see below my blizzard preparation list from yesterday. I know your snow-removal trucks are working hard this morning to clean up the foot and a half of snow that fell last night. I know there are lots of roads to clear. But if at all possible, could you please speed one of your guys over to our neighborhood before this house ends up looking like a violent crime scene?

Thanks,

Jenny

BLIZZARD PREP LIST

~~Milk~~	~~Snacks~~
~~Bread~~	~~Batteries~~
~~Eggs~~	~~Water~~
~~Wine~~	Tampons
~~Toilet paper~~	~~Ice melt~~
~~Diapers~~	~~Gas for snowblower~~
~~Baby wipes~~	
~~Paper towels~~	

Infant Sleep Manual: A Compilation of the Best Professional Wisdom

(1) If your baby is significantly under six months of age, it's impossible for you to spoil him or her. You should respond to cries promptly and do whatever it takes to help your baby sleep. [Note that whatever soothing method you choose could cause your child to become dependent on you to get to sleep and return to sleep during normal sleep-cycle wakings. Your method of helping your baby fall asleep and stay asleep will transform into a troublesome crutch anywhere between two weeks of age and six months of age.]

(2) Some ways to soothe your baby include:

> a) tight swaddling (See Warning 2a below)
> b) white noise or shushing sounds (See Warning 2b below)
> c) swinging or rocking (See Warning 2c below)
> d) offering something for the baby to suck (See

Warning 2d below)

e) wearing your baby in a sling or pouch (See Warning 2e below)

f) sleeping with your baby (See Warning 2f below)

Warning 2a: You can keep your child swaddled up to 20 hours each day. Note that doing so may stunt your child's growth and prevent him from discovering how to self-soothe by sucking on his fingers. Note also that at least five people a day will comment to you that your child must be overheating. Even if your child cries when being swaddled, don't worry. He probably loves it but just needs a few minutes to realize that swaddling means he's about to be soothed and happy. Note that there is no way to know if he's crying because he hasn't realized he loves it or if he's crying because it's driving him bat-shit crazy to be hog-tied.

Warning 2b: Some babies are unable to sleep because they're overstimulated, in which case white noise will help drown out auditory stimuli. However, some babies are unable to sleep because they're understimulated. These babies will be better able to sleep if you expose them to the same household noises that lulled them while in utero. There is no way to know which kind of baby you have, because by the time you experiment with both ways, both kinds of babies will be freaking out crying from being overtired. Note that many experts believe babies sleep in loud environs because of something called habituation: That is, when overloaded by too much stimuli, they conk out. They do not get good quality sleep while habituating. Your parents and grandparents, as well as friends who've birthed portable/easy sleepers, will think you're crazy if you tell them about this very real phenomenon. These folks are deserving of a phone call from you at each of your baby's extra five or six wakings throughout the nights that follow habituation sleep. Put them on auto-dial.

Warning 2c: Many babies love to swing, but it is advised that you swing them in a forward/backward motion rather than side-to-side, to emulate the motion they felt in utero when mom was walking. Babies do not get motion sickness, although the two cups of breast milk or formula they upchuck while in a swing may lead you to believe otherwise. Never put a crying baby into a swing; soothe him first and then put him in the swing on the highest setting, preferably in a tight swaddle (see warning 2a about swaddling, above). Note that swing sleep and other sleep during motion is NOT quality sleep. Studies show it is actually non-restorative sleep, and thus, while your baby will at least have his screaming milkhole quieted for a period of time, he will actually be recharging his body for an extra hour of fussy time, on top of the three hours of fussy time he already has planned for you each night.

Warning 2d: Babies typically need to spend about 80 percent of their awake time sucking—on their hands, on pacifiers, on bottles, and/or on mom's breast. During the first few months, when it's impossible to spoil your baby, you should not worry about letting him or her fall asleep while at the breast or bottle. This a soothing, bonding, wonderful time for you and baby! After he is three months and one day, however, it becomes a bad habit that interferes with your child's ability to sleep. Note that it does not qualify as a bad habit until three months and one day—or, if you subscribe to more lax experts' advice, until four or six months and one day. If you find that your baby can fall asleep only while nursing, you probably should have awoken him after he fell asleep at the breast all through those early weeks and then laid him down awake but drowsy. Hindsight!

Warning 2e: Wearing your baby is a great way to bond, help him sleep, and still get things done! Note that the safest and most soothing position for infants in 95 percent of slings, pouches, wraps, and other carriers is with his bobbing face smashed up against your breasts in some fashion that causes him to root. Go ahead and nurse him when he wakes. This will probably be every 10-15 minutes for the first few months or more. Some wraps are so complicated that it may take you a half-hour to get your crying baby into them, but your baby will almost undoubtedly crash to sleep once situated and done nursing from the breast that's now two inches from his milk-divining nose. (See note in Warning 2c about motion sleeping. You are in for one hell of a night.)

Warning 2f: If you're obese or have been drinking,

you are going to roll over on your baby and smother him. It's only a matter of time. Otherwise, take that baby into your bed and help him sleep! Note that after three months of age, he will begin to wake more frequently—as often as every hour— to nurse or play. You will not be able to move him into his own bed until he's eleven. Unless you haven't weaned him by then, which according to attachment-parenting demagogue Dr. William Sears, is fine.

(3) Always sleep baby on his back, to prevent SIDS—the D of which stands for *death*, by the way. D-E-A-T-H. Providing your baby with tummy time is necessary during other hours of the day, to ensure he doesn't develop a flat spot on the back of his head. Your baby will likely writhe and cry in horror when placed on his belly, lifting limbs and head as though he's skydiving, can't open his chute, and is afraid of heights, *unless you are placing him on his belly when he is sleepy.* In that case, the baby will settle quickly and sleep twice as long as would otherwise be possible. This is really just an aside, because you are NOT to sleep the baby on his or her belly. Unless he has reflux. Then you are to sleep him on his side or, if your pediatrician is in a certain camp of pediatricians, on his belly. Note that if you do

this, he will have less pain from reflux but could possibly DIE from SIDS. Do not sleep your baby in his car seat. He likes to sleep there, but he could die. Of SIDS. Also, when you put baby down on his back, be prepared for his rubbery arms to flail uncontrollably due to the Moro reflex, which will wake him completely, unless you are swaddling (see Warning 2a, above, about swaddling). Swaddling too tightly in too many clothes can lead to overheating, which can put your child at risk of DYING from SIDS.

(4) Keep awake times brief. Most babies under three months of age can tolerate no more than one to two hours of awake time between sleeping times. Some can tolerate only 30 minutes for the first many months. Experts say you should watch for sleepy cues, like yawning, finger-sucking, hiccupping, faraway-look gazing, and various other behaviors that all babies exhibit at all times, even when not tired. You must take shots in the dark to discern how much awake time your child can take. If you wait too long, your baby will be overtired and very difficult to soothe. If you don't wait long enough, your baby will be pissed that you're swaddling him again and not letting him get some quiet-alert time already, and he will cry and appear overtired.

(5) Don't worry about doing whatever it takes to help your young baby sleep! When he's old enough—and only God knows when that will be –he'll be rested enough that you can teach him to sleep independently. According to various experts, this "sleep training" is best done at six months (Ferber). Or four months (Weissbluth). Or twelve weeks (Hogg, Mindell, et al). We recommend starting at twelve weeks, three days, and two-and-quarter hours. Then again, the best time to begin is when the baby has developed some self-soothing abilities, typically between three and four months (Weissbluth). By that time bad habits will have already developed (Hogg, Mindell, West, et al). Another option is to wait until the baby's brain has matured and naturally begun to organize his sleep into longer stretches, around sixteen weeks (Weissbluth). Note that dependency habits are usually in place ten weeks before that (Mindell, West, et al). Many experts recommend starting sleep training at six weeks, which also happens to be the peak of babies' fussiness and wakefulness. Remember you can't really form bad habits during the first three months, unless you subscribe to the *Babywise* philosophy, in which case you should know you created the bad habits while the baby was still in utero— and should break them immediately after he crowns.

You can teach your co-dependent child to sleep independently by putting him down drowsy but awake. You can pat and shush him to soothe him, but don't pick him up. Or do pick him up if he is getting hysterical, though this will be giving him intermittent reinforcement and make the sleep training take three times as long. You could also leave him to cry and check on him at 15-minute intervals—or 3-minute intervals, if you don't want him to feel abandoned, which he will because you're doing it all wrong. Note that such repeated reappearances will likely hype some babies up and make the crying last longer.

Don't start any sort of sleep training program unless you're ready to be consistent with it and have nerves of steel. (To test your nerves, ask yourself: Could I cut off the ears of a live kitten, with dull cutlery, *for a worthy cause*?) Baby may barf while crying. This is just to get your attention and should be casually cleaned up. Or it may be because he's too young to be sleep trained, in which case you're a fucking monster. You should wait until he's six months old to try again, or three months old, or—you know what? Blast it. Just put him on your breast, pour yourself a glass of wine, and try to survive.

15 Pat Answers

1. A washcloth

2. Legume-heavy dinners

3. Not shaving

4. Sharing too much with my husband about my toileting

5. Panties I've owned and worn for 10 years

6. Ankle cellulite

7. That nagging sense of shame that even marriage can't kill

8. My winning personality

9. Lots of red wine

10. Good marksmanship

11. Religion

12. Preschool politics

13. Post-partum depression

14. Sweet, sweet luck

15. The audacity of hope

Originally titled:

Things I Considered Saying When My Gynecologist Asked What I'll Be Using for Birth Control

A Lesson in Country Circumcision

Our home is basically a mullet: business in the front, party in the back. The front faces a manicured suburban avenue of empty-nesters endlessly mowing and hedge-trimming. Our backyard spills into a vast expanse of corn and soy crops belonging to old farmers, so our kids are forever shedding their clothes to play naked and wild back there.

As honorary country folk, we're the proud owners of five hens. We bought them as day-old chicks, and the kids used to hold them in their cupped hands for hours, giggling at the ticklish pecks from barely-there beaks. While the birds lost their fuzz and grew pin feathers in a brooder, my husband toiled away building a coop:

When the hens moved outside, the kids really missed having them in the house. They'd visit the girls often, marveling at what I'd promised they'd see: Grown hens eat ANYTHING, including cooked chicken and their own cracked-open eggs. The kids often smashed grass against the wiry hardware cloth, and the hens would rush over like famished POWs, violently plucking with their sharp beaks.

Gradually we started bringing them people food. They loved spaghetti and scrambled eggs. Bread crumbs? Check. Mango? Yup. Ravioli? For sure. Anything pressed against the coop was gobbled with reckless abandon.

One day I decided to show my 3-year-old how to dig worms up from our garden. Worms are like living spaghetti to chickens, and while I love all creatures great and small, I knew my son would marvel at seeing the food-chain in action. His little elbows looked so darn cute digging away. His plump buns made me laugh as he raced over to dangle worms through the hardware cloth. He was reticent about getting his fingers pecked, so I reassured him not to worry, that it wouldn't hurt the rough pads of his fingertips.

Resuming my digging, I looked back just as my son was—what the illogical HELL!?—preparing to push his penis against the coop! Kids do the darndest things, you say? No, they do the dumbest things. I could see the wheels turning in his head. You know what I mean: What happens if I push this button on this toy? What happens if I keep dropping my fork? What happens if I put this bead in my nosehole?

"NoooooOOOOoOoo!" I screamed. "Don't feed your penis to the chickens!"

He jumped back as if woken from a trance. I could read on his face that lingering expression of *what would have happened?* So, I spelled it all out for him, how the chickens would have violently poked and torn at his penis.

"Like a worm?" he said, the whites now showing all around the irises of his eyes.

"Like a worm," I answered, my heart still pounding. Considering those embarrassingly steamy Google searches and chat-room forays I made when deciding not to circumcise my son, perish the thought of it all meeting such a gruesome and wasteful end! I'm so glad to say my son never attempted this daring feat again. Yes, thanks again to me, everything's still intact. And as for that party out back? You can bet it's still going strong.

Acknowledgements

Thank you first and foremost to my best friend and husband, Blaine. You literally gave me the material that made this book possible, and there's been no greater gift in my life than our children. You're a rare and dying breed. I love that you always tell me the truth about what I write, despite the negative correlation this honesty sometimes has to your sex life.

Thank you also to my kids, the sunshine of my life, though you won't be able to read this acknowledgement until you're older due to the preceding sentence. Everything I have ever written about you has been written with love, even the booger stuff. Shine on, you crazy little diamonds.

A huge thank you to my parents. Motherhood has taught me how much you love me, and why you keep saying *you could write a book, why don't you write that book,* and *we're so disappointed in you for not writing that book.* Okay, you didn't say that last one. The mother in me understands it all now, how much you want your kids to reach their dreams. Thank you for helping me to do that.

Special thanks to my loyal readers at The Momplex blog; to my fourth-grade teacher Mrs. Paula Yingst, my first and longest lasting supporter; and to Ann Edmunds, the person whose words rattled me into believing I could do this thing. Thank you to Meredith Maslich at Possibilities Publishing. You are a quintessential professional and opened the door to my dreams. Last but not least, I wish to thank the smart, funny, and compassionate women who kept me from leaping out windows in the early years of motherhood, my beloved Living Room Ladies: Lynn Cociani, Mary Lui, Pamela Budin-Pereira, and Shiloh Smith-Wittwer. We all got our lives back after all, didn't we?

Made in the USA
Lexington, KY
11 April 2013